CATCH FISH NOW!

in the

FLORIDA *PANHANDLE*

Written by

Mike Babbidge

Disclaimer

The Florida and Federal fishing regulations summarized in the Appendix to this book are subject to change at any time. Currently applicable bag limits are particularly dynamic in nature. Accordingly, the reader should stay tuned to developments to ensure full compliance with the law.

The LORAN coordinates contained in this book are uncorrected for plotting on navigational charts. Also, due to the varying reporting approach used by local artificial reef programs, there is no guarantee that the numbers provided correspond to the center of the deployed material. Finally, as a result of Hurricanes Erin and Opal (1995), some bottom structure has experienced movement and/or modification of previous bottom relief characteristics due to excessive silting.

Published by

BABBCO ENTERPRISES
117 Racetrack Road, #204
Fort Walton Beach, FL 32547

In conjunction with
Computer Publishing Group, Inc.
Holley Plaza 6904 Navarre Pkwy., Ste. A
Navarre, FL 32566

Printed in the United States of America

CATCH FISH NOW!
in the
FLORIDA *PANHANDLE*

Table of Contents

List of Figures

If you wish to be happy
    for one hour
        get intoxicated.

If you wish to be happy
    for three days,
        get married.

If you wish to be happy
    for eight days,
        kill your pig and eat it.

If you wish to be happy
    forever,
        learn to fish.

Ancient Chinese Proverb

CHAPTER 1

ANGLING OVERVIEW OF THE *PANHANDLE*

This book is the first in a planned series of geographically oriented books on Florida saltwater fishing. It covers the area and kinds of fishing highlighted below:

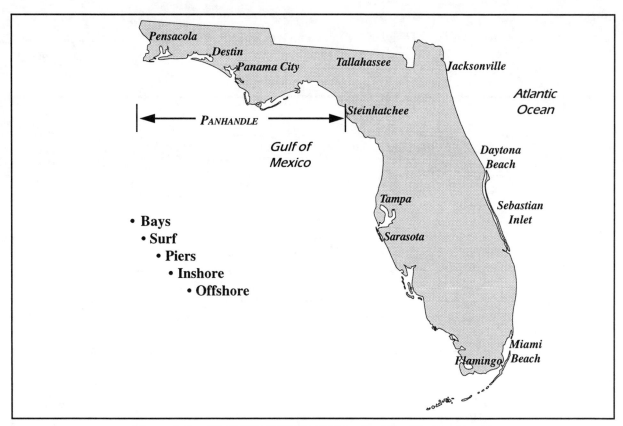

Figure 1.0 - **CATCH FISH NOW! in the Florida *Panhandle***

CATCH FISH NOW! is designed to give you the information you need to enjoy immediate fishing success in ***Panhandle*** waters. It answers the following basic questions:

- What's biting?
- When and where does it bite?
- How do you rig up to catch it?
- What kind of tackle is required?

In the process, it provides an abundance of proven "how to" information and "hot tips" to give you an edge on the "catching part" of fishing.

The Florida ***Panhandle*** as defined in **CATCH FISH NOW!** includes some 270 miles of coastline from the

Florida-Alabama border in the West to the fishing village of Steinhatchee to the East. In between, there are many prime areas to **CATCH FISH NOW!** - at any time of year. These include:

- Over 100 miles of potentially fishable surf.
- Thirteen bays with adjacent bayous, inlets and coves.
- Many river deltas, connecting creeks, and passes to the Gulf.
- An abundance of capes, islands, flats, bridges, piers, channels and submerged structure.
- Superb inshore and offshore natural and man-made spots in the Gulf of Mexico.

Many world records for a variety of saltwater gamefish have been set in Florida ***Panhandle*** waters.

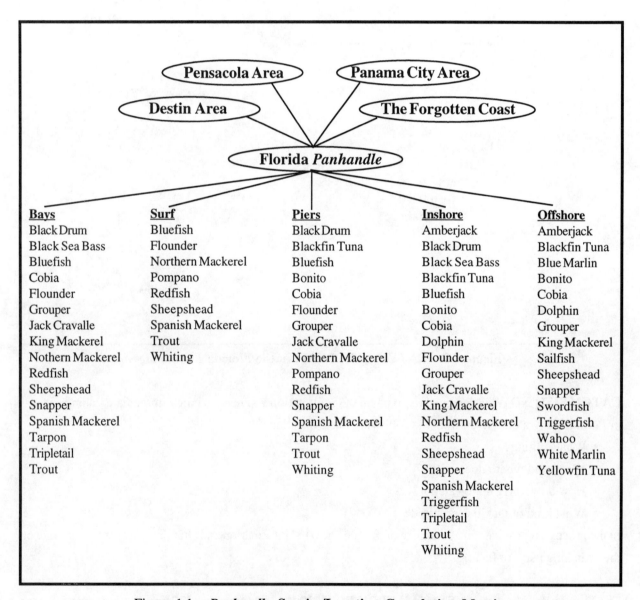

Bays
Black Drum
Black Sea Bass
Bluefish
Cobia
Flounder
Grouper
Jack Cravalle
King Mackerel
Nothern Mackerel
Redfish
Sheepshead
Snapper
Spanish Mackerel
Tarpon
Tripletail
Trout

Surf
Bluefish
Flounder
Northern Mackerel
Pompano
Redfish
Sheepshead
Spanish Mackerel
Trout
Whiting

Piers
Black Drum
Blackfin Tuna
Bluefish
Bonito
Cobia
Flounder
Grouper
Jack Cravalle
Northern Mackerel
Pompano
Redfish
Snapper
Spanish Mackerel
Tarpon
Trout
Whiting

Inshore
Amberjack
Black Drum
Black Sea Bass
Blackfin Tuna
Bluefish
Bonito
Cobia
Dolphin
Flounder
Grouper
Jack Cravalle
King Mackerel
Northern Mackerel
Redfish
Sheepshead
Snapper
Spanish Mackerel
Triggerfish
Tripletail
Trout
Whiting

Offshore
Amberjack
Blackfin Tuna
Blue Marlin
Bonito
Cobia
Dolphin
Grouper
King Mackerel
Sailfish
Sheepshead
Snapper
Swordfish
Triggerfish
Wahoo
White Marlin
Yellowfin Tuna

Figure 1.1 - ***Panhandle*** **Species/Location Correlation Matrix**

Fishing diversity in the **Panhandle** is equally impressive in two respects. First, there are about 30 kinds of gamefish available in the area. Second, there are a number of different areas where the same kind of fish may be caught at any given time. This is highlighted in Figure 1.1.

The data presented in the figure provides useful insights. It correctly suggests, for example, that if it's too rough to get out in the Gulf for some small boat inshore trolling for King Mackerel, they can also be caught off area piers and in at least two **Panhandle** bays. Flounder provide another good example. At several times during the year, these fish may be caught inshore by bottom fishing on structure, drifting or anchored in a bay, off one of the area's piers, and more often than not, in the surf. Two important points should be made. First, the matrix is a generalization. The fish shown for each location are only the most commonly caught species. Now and then, other species show up for surprise visits. Sailfish have been hooked and landed from area piers. Cobia and King Mackerel are both caught in some of the bays in the area. And, Grouper can be caught with some consistency in all area bays if you know where to fish. But, in every case, these are exceptions to what a fisherman should expect. The second important point about the matrix is that it addresses only what are usually considered gamefish. There are other species available that are fun to catch and, in some cases, good to eat, too. Sharks, Sailcats, Ladyfish, Pinfish, Grunts, and a variety of Jacks fall into this category. They too, can be caught with regularity in **Panhandle** waters.

Now, with the generalities out of the way, what kind of fish can you expect to catch at any particular time during the year? Or, asked another way, at any particular time of the year, what kinds of fish are usually biting somewhere in the **Panhandle** area? Figure 1.2 can be used to answer both questions. The indicated activity is a combination of the individual area data contained in Figures 2.2, 2.11, 2.20, and 2.29.

The data in the summary was synthesized from the fishing reports published in **Panhandle** newspapers and other publications over the last several years. The information in the reports usually comes from area bait and tackle stores, marinas, lodges and landings.

The fish identified on the left hand side of the table are those most frequently caught in **Panhandle** waters. Other species of lesser sport or eating value, while also present in significant quantities, have been omitted for the sake of brevity. Blanks in the table represent no reported catches of the species during the month. Although the fish may have been present, people weren't fishing for them because the weather didn't cooperate, other kinds of fish were just biting too well, or fishermen were just not fishing.

Although a summary like figure 1.2 provides useful insights into what bites when, it can't tell you what happened yesterday or what might happen today. Fortunately, there are a number of other sources of current fishing information readily available to **Panhandle** area fisherman. These include the following:

Panhandle Gamefish	J	F	M	A	M	J	J	A	S	O	N	D
Amberjack	X	X	XX	XX	XXX	XX	XXX	XXX	XXX	XX	X	X
Black Drum	XX	XXX	XX	XX	X	XXX	X	XX	XX	XX	XX	XX
Black Sea Bass	XX	XX	X	XX	XX	XX	X	X	X	X	X	XX
Blackfin Tuna	X		X	X	XX	XX	XX	X	XX	XX	X	
Bluefish	X	X	X	X	XX	XX	XXX	XX	X	X	X	X
Blue Marlin				X	XX	XX	XX	XX	X			
Bonito	X			XX	XXX	XX	XXX	XXX	XX	XX	X	
Cobia			X	XXX	XXX	XXX	XX	XX	XX	X		
Dolphin				X	XX	XX	XXX	XX	XXX	X	X	
Flounder	X	X	X	XX	XX	XX	X	XX	XXX	XX	XX	XXX
Grouper	X	XX	XX	XX	XX	XX	XX	XX	XX	XX	X	X
Jack Cravalle			X	X	X	XX	XXX	XXX	XX	X	X	
King Mackerel				X	XX	XXX	XXX	XXX	XX	XX	X	
Northern Mackerel		X	X	XX	XX	XXX	XX	X	X	X	X	
Pompano		X	X	XXX	XXX	XX	X	X	X	X		
Redfish	X	X	XX	XX	XXX	XXX	XXX	XXX	XX	XX	XX	X
Sailfish						X	X	XX	XX	X	X	
Sheepshead	XX	XX	XX	XXX	XXX	XX	XXX	XX	XX	XX	XX	XXX
Snapper	X	X	XX	XX	XX	XX	XX	XX	XX	XX	XX	X
Spanish Mackerel		X	X	XXX	XXX	XXX	XXX	XX	XX	XX	X	
Swordfish								X	X			
Tarpon				X	XXX	XX	XXX	XX	X			
Triggerfish	X	X	XX	XX	XX	XXX	XX	XX	X	XX	X	
Tripletail				X	XX	XX	XX					
Trout	X	X	XX	XX	XXX	XX	XX	XX	XXX	XX	XX	X
Wahoo				X	XX	XX	XX	XX	X			
White Marlin						X	XX	XX	X	X		
Whiting			X	X	XX	XXX	XXX	XX	XX	X	X	
Yellowfin Tuna						X	XX	XX	XX	X		

Legend: Blank= No reported activity   XX= Good catches reported during the month

X= At least a few reported caught in the area during the month   XXX= Great. Even if you just do a few things right, you're going to catch fish

Figure 1.2 - *Panhandle* Fishing Activity Summary

- *Pensacola News Journal.* This newspaper publishes a fishing report every Monday.
- *The Northwest Florida Daily News* (Destin area). This newspaper publishes a superb outdoor column and area fishing report every Friday.
- *Destin Log.* This paper, which is published twice a week, provides a fishing report on Wednesdays and photos of notable charter boat catches on both Wednesday and Saturday.
- *The News Herald* (Panama City area). This newspaper publishes articles on fishing on Tuesdays and an excellent fishing activity report on Fridays.
- *Area bait and tackle stores.* All of these are usually excellent sources of current fishing information.
- *Panhandle Area Docks.* Another way to find out what's biting is to visit the docks where the party and charter boats come in from their daily trips. Return times vary for these boats, but the half-day trips usually start returning to port between 11 a.m. and Noon and all-day trips between 4 and 5 p.m.
- *VHF Radio.* A final very timely way to determine local fishing activity is to monitor a VHF radio. Almost all boats now rely on VHF radio for boat-to-boat and boat-to-shore communication, so listening to the almost continuous traffic can provide very current information. A number of different frequencies are usually in use, but channel 68 is a good place to start your monitoring. According to the Federal Communications Commission, other channels of interest might include: Emergency - #16; other recreational boater channels - #'s 9, 69, 71, 72, and 78; working channels for commercial boats only - #'s 1, 7, 8, 9, 10, 11, 18, 19, 63, 67, 79, 80, and 88; and, marine operator - #'s 24-28, 84, 85, 86, and 87.

Before getting down to specifics, it is important to note one general caveat related to the LORAN numbers that will be presented throughout this book. As you may know, the *Panhandle* area experienced two major hurricanes during the 1995 hurricane season. Based on subsequent diver's and other reports, it's clear that these storm significantly affected the location of smaller artificial structures (tires, car bodies, etc.) in 100 or less feet of water. While larger artificial or deeper, smaller structures were not moved significantly, they, too, were affected by the storms. Specifically, there has been a build-up of silt at many sites so relief from the bottom will now appear differently when viewed on a bottom machine. The answer here is simple. Use LORAN numbers as a starting point--and keep your bottom machine on and tracking at all times!

So, with that overview of *Panhandle* area fishing as background, it's time to get serious. There are fish out there waiting to be caught by you! The remainder of this book is designed to help you do exactly that. Chapter 2 addresses when and where to fish in the Florida *Panhandle*. Chapter 3 describes how to catch each of the gamefish that may be available at any given time in this area. Chapter 4 follows with special subjects that may be of interest to you including: Fishing for the Younger Set, Crabbing for the Entire Family, Saltwater Fly-fishing and *Panhandle* Scalloping. **CATCH FISH NOW!** concludes with an appendix covering currently applicable fishing regulations. So, with all that in mind, it's time to **CATCH FISH NOW!** in the waters of the Florida *Panhandle*.

—PERSONAL NOTES —

CHAPTER 2

WHEN AND WHERE TO FISH

For presentation purposes, the Florida *Panhandle* has been divided into the four segments shown in Figure 2.0. Although this division is purely arbitrary, it does provide a relatively simple framework for our discussion on how to **CATCH FISH NOW!** in the *Panhandle*. We'll start our discussion in the West at the Alabama state line and work our way East some 270 miles to the fishing village of Steinhatchee. In the process, each of the subjects listed in the Presentation Format column will be addressed.

Presentation Format	Florida *Panhandle*			
	PENSACOLA AREA Alabama line to Navarre Beach	DESTIN AREA Navarre Beach to Inlet Beach	PANAMA CITY AREA Inlet Beach to Tyndall Air Force Base	FORGOTTEN COAST Mexico Beach to Steinhatchee
Annual Fishing Summary	✓	✓	✓	✓
Monthly Catch Data	✓	✓	✓	✓
Bays	✓	✓	✓	✓
Surf	✓	✓	✓	no
Piers	no	✓	✓	no
Inshore	✓	✓	✓	✓
Offshore • **Big Game** • **Bottom**	✓ ✓	(Desoto Canyon) → ✓	✓	no ✓

Figure 2.0 - **Chapter 2 Organization**

Before we get started on when and where to fish in the *Panhandle*, a couple of words about the format exceptions noted in Figure 2.0 may be of interest:

- First, the Pensacola area no longer has any operative gulf fishing piers. In 1995, hurricanes Erin and Opal destroyed both the Pensacola Beach and Navarre Beach piers.
- Second, since the Pensacola, Destin, and Panama City areas all have ready access to Desoto Canyon Offshore waters, coverage of that area will only be presented once -- in the Pensacola section of the chapter.

- Finally, the section on the Forgotten Coast only contains passing references to Surf, Piers, and Offshore big game trolling. In order, this is a recognition that: 1) there really isn't any along the Forgotten Coast; 2) the piers that exist do not provide access to Inshore gulf species; and, 3) big game trolling 85-100 miles out isn't an important part of Forgotten Coast sportfishing.

So much for the content and format of this chapter. It's now time to talk about when and where to fish. As you review the following material, be sure to check the similar writeups for areas adjacent to the one you intend to fish. In many cases, there is considerable overlap since the definition of the four ***Panhandle*** areas was purely arbitrary.

— PERSONAL NOTES —

PENSACOLA AREA

Located in the western-most part of the Florida **Panhandle**, the Pensacola area offers unlimited opportunities for good fishing year round. As you can see below, the area has several large bays, with rivers and creeks that feed into them. It also has a section of Santa Rosa Sound that serves as the Intercoastal Waterway. The area is further enhanced with roughly 35 miles of Gulf beaches, a Pass into the Gulf, and only a 30 mile run to the superb Offshore fishing grounds in the Desoto Canyon area.

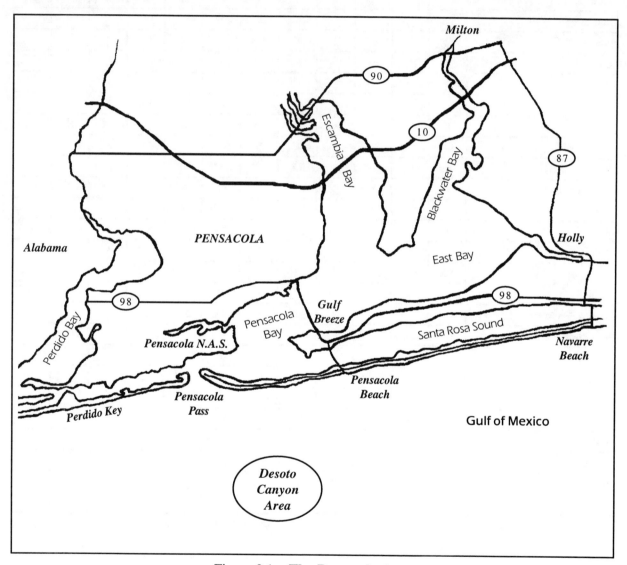

Figure 2.1 - **The Pensacola Area**

The following figure reflects what Pensacola area fishermen have caught (or said they caught) on a monthly basis over the last several years.

Panhandle Gamefish	Historic Monthly Activity											
	J	**F**	**M**	**A**	**M**	**J**	**J**	**A**	**S**	**O**	**N**	**D**
Amberjack	X	X	X	X	X	XX	XXX	XXX	XX	X	X	X
Black Drum	X	XX	XX	XX		X	X	X	XX	X	XX	X
Black Sea Bass												
Blackfin Tuna	X		X		XX	X	X	X	XX	X		
Bluefish	X	X	X	X	X	X	X	X	X	X		X
Blue Marlin						X	X	XX	X	X		
Bonito					X	X	XX	X	XX	X		
Cobia			X	XX	XXX	XX	X	X	X			
Dolphin					X	X	XX	XX	XXX	X		
Flounder			X	X	X	X	XX	XX	XX	X	XX	X
Grouper	X	XX	XX	X	X	XX	X	X	X	XX	X	X
Jack Cravalle			X	X	X	XX	XXX	XX	X			
King Mackerel			X	XX	XXX	XXX	XX	XX				
Northern Mackerel		X	X		XX	X	XX	X	X			
Pompano			X	XX	XX	X	X	X	X			
Redfish	X	X	XX	XX	XX	XX	XX	X	XX	X	X	X
Sailfish						X	X	XX	XX	X		
Sheepshead	XX	XX	XX	X	X	X	X	X	XX	X	XX	XX
Snapper	X	X	XX	XX	X	X	X	XX	X			
Spanish Mackerel			X	XX	XX	XXX	XX	XX	XX			
Swordfish									X	X		
Tarpon						X	X					
Triggerfish	X	X	XX	X	X	XX	X	X	X	X		
Tripletail						X						
Trout	X	X	XX	XX	XX	XX	XX	X	XX	XX	X	X
Wahoo						X	X	XX	X	XX	X	
White Marlin						X	XX	X	X			
Whiting			X	X	XX	X	XXX	XX	X	X		
Yellowfin Tuna						X	X	X	XX	X		

Legend: Blank= No reported activity   XX= Good catches reported during the month

X= At least a few reported caught in the area during the month   XXX= Great. Even if you just do a few things right, you're going to catch fish

Figure 2.2 - **Pensacola Area Annual Fishing Summary**

The monthly fishing activity presented above has necessarily been generalized. Even so, it provides useful insights into when you can reasonably expect to catch a particular kind of fish--or what kind of fish you can expect to catch in any given month. For example, in any given year, you can generally expect to catch Speckled or White Trout somewhere in the Pensacola area every month of the year. Pompano, on the other hand, usually only show up during the months of March through September. The following narrative sharpens up this generalized focus. It describes area fishing activity on a month-by-month basis using specific catch data obtained from area tackle stores, landings, etc. The locations identified in the data will be highlighted in the maps and charts that follow.

January
- Blackfin Tuna Offshore.
- Redfish (Reds) and Speckled Trout (Specs) in the East River.
- Sheepshead and White Trout off the Three Mile and Bob Sikes bridges.
- White Trout in East Bay below the mouth of the Blackwater River.
- Grouper and Snapper in 60-100 feet of water Offshore.

February
- Specs and Reds in Blackwater River holes at Milton.
- Sheepshead on all area bridges.
- Grouper and Snapper on Offshore spots in over 140 feet of water.
- Grouper on structure in Pensacola Bay deep water holes.

March
- Cobia starting to show along the beach.
- Gag Grouper in 180 feet of water Offshore.
- Sheepshead all over Navarre bridge.
- Pompano around the remains of the Pensacola Beach pier.
- Specs, Reds, and Flounder at the East Bay "power lines".
- Reds and Sheepshead at Ft. Pickens.
- Red and Black Snapper on wrecks and reefs in 50-90 feet of water.
- Specs spreading out over all grass flats.
- Pompano begin to show along all beaches.
- Specs off the "rock piles" on both sides of the Three Mile bridge.

April
- Cobia and Pompano along the beaches.
- Spawning Specs on the flats.
- King Mackerel (Kings) starting to show Inshore.
- Spanish Mackerel (Spanish) around Pensacola Pass jetties and Inshore along the beaches.
- Specs on the rock piles on the South side of Three Mile bridge.
- Cobia, Spanish, Pompano, Bluefish (Blues), Bonito and Jack Cravalle off the currently inoperative Navarre pier.
- Spanish in Santa Rosa Sound around Ft. Pickens and off Three Mile and Bob Sikes bridges.

May
- Specs on all area grass flats.
- Kings over Inshore structure.
- Sheepshead, Specs, White Trout and Reds at the East Bay "power lines".

- Cobia and Pompano along the beaches.
- Spanish off Three Mile and Bob Sikes bridges and at Ft. Pickens.

June
- Kings over Inshore structure.
- Spanish everywhere.
- Blue and White Marlin, bull and schoolie Dolphin, Yellowfin Tuna and Wahoo begin to show Offshore.
- King Mackerel off the Bayfront Auditorium.
- Grouper in Escambia Bay on structure in 25-40 feet of water.
- A Tripletail caught off the Three Mile bridge.
- Specs and Reds at the East Bay "power lines".
- Tarpon starting to show off the remains of the Pensacola Beach pier.

July
- Spanish, Jack Cravalle, Tarpon, Specs, White Trout, Reds, Flounder and Black Drum from Three Mile and Bob Sikes bridges.
- Kings from Three Mile bridge.
- Kings, Spanish, Bonito and Flounder at Ft. Pickens.
- Schoolie Dolphin along weedlines.
- Grouper, Snapper and Triggerfish (Triggers) in less than 100 feet of water.
- Blue and White Marlin, Sailfish, Wahoo and Yellowfin Tuna Offshore.

August
- Blue and White Marlin, Yellowfin and Blackfin Tuna, Sailfish and Wahoo Offshore.
- Specs, Reds, Flounder, Sheepshead, Black Drum, Kings and Spanish widely scattered over the area.
- Specs and Flounder in the Blackwater River at Milton and the I-10 bridge

September
- Flounder in Escambia Bay and the Blackwater River.
- Kings, Spanish, Blackfin Tuna, Blacktip Sharks and Pompano in the area of the old Pensacola Beach pier.
- Kings and Spanish remain good off Bob Sikes and Three Mile bridges.
- Kings, Spanish and Flounder at Ft. Pickens.
- Reds and Specs on grass flats and Three Mile bridge rock piles.

October
- Blue and White Marlin Offshore.
- Warsaw Grouper and Red Snapper in 300+ feet of water.
- Reds, Specs, White Trout, Flounder, Blues, Black Drum and Sheepshead widely scattered over the area.

November
- Specs, White Trout, Sheepshead, Flounder, Reds and Black Drum at the East Bay "power lines".
- Bull Reds at the Pensacola Pass/Ft. Pickens.
- Specs and Reds into the Blackwater and Escher systems.
- Flounder, Reds, Black Drum, Specs and Blues at Three Mile and Bob Sikes bridges.

December

- Specs in the East River.
- Reds and Sheepshead at the East Bay "power lines".
- Specs, White Trout, Reds, Flounder and Sheepshead at the Three Mile bridge rock piles.

With that top level look at what bites when in mind, it's now time to get more specific about where to fish. The following will focus on the five generic kinds of fishing in the Pensacola area. In the process, maps, charts, and navigation data will be presented to help you find good spots to fish. Pensacola area bays and adjacent waters will be described first.

Bays

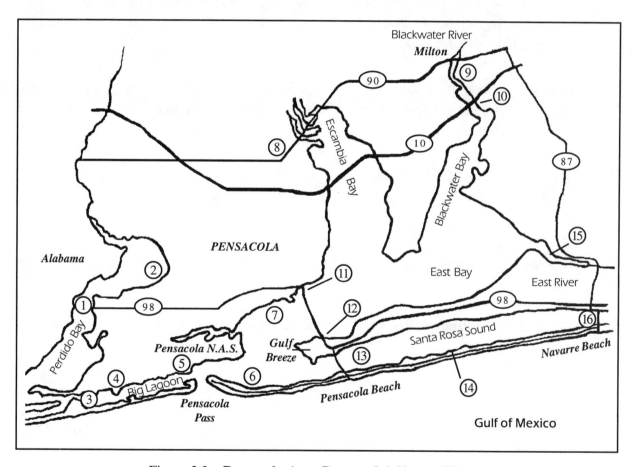

Figure 2.3 - **Pensacola Area Bays and Adjacent Waters**

Legend

① Highway 98 bridge pilings. Productive deep and shallow water fishing. Sheepshead in the Winter and Specs and Reds Spring/Summer.

② Roadside water access to Perdido Bay. Good shore fishing into an extensive area of old pilings.

③   Perdido Key/Johnson Beach segment of Gulf Islands National Seashore. Good access to the flats along the Intercoastal Waterway/Big Lagoon. Four dollars per car entrance fee that's good for seven days.

④   Big Lagoon State Recreation Area. Entrance off SR 293 and fee of $3.25 per car (up to eight people). Good boat ramps. Superior wade fishing on the grass flats off the southeast shore of the park.

⑤   Naval Air Station (NAS) Pensacola. Access to the Air Station is not controlled except during Defense emergencies. Two areas may be of interest. One is the Marina at Sherman Cove. It's located on the Southwest side of the NAS and has excellent boat ramps. There's a nice beach with ready access to the Intercoastal Waterway just East of the Marina. Farther on East on Radford Blvd., in the industrial part of the NAS, there is a half-mile or so of bulkheaded shoreline. Deep water (and big fish) can be found along this stretch.

⑥   Ft. Pickens segment of the Gulf Islands National Seashore. Pensacola Pass jetty access. Also easy access to the superb flats along the North shore. An entrance fee of $4.00 per car is charged and is good for seven days.

⑦   Municipal Pier/Bayfront Auditorium. Deep water fishing with close-by parking is available around the perimeter of the downtown Pensacola Convention Center. Among other species, King Mackerel in the late Summer.

⑧   Boat ramps on either side of the Highway 90 bridge over the Escambia River. Good structure fishing in the river.

⑨   During the Nov-Feb period, Specs and Reds can be found in deep water holes in the Blackwater River at Milton.

⑩   I-10 Bridge. Good fishing around the deep water pilings.

⑪⑫   Pensacola Bay Bridge (called "Three Mile" bridge in local fishing reports). The Old Bay bridge, which parallels the new bridge on its East side, has been turned into two fishing piers. One pier is accessible on the Pensacola side from the Wayside Park/Visitor Center that is located there. This section of the old bridge is limited to foot access only, there is no charge to fish and a fishing license is required by non-residents. There are submerged "rockpiles" on both sides of this pier near the North shore. The other segment of the old bridge is accessible from the Gulf Breeze end. This pier is open 24 hours a day except during periods of inclement weather. Cost is $3.00 for driver and car and $2.00 for each additional passenger. Children under 13 are free. No fishing license is required for non-residents. This segment also has submerged "rockpiles" on both sides of the pier, just off the South shore.

⑬   Bob Sikes Bridge. (Also called Pensacola Beach Road on some maps). An old bridge parallels the new bridge on its east side and is accessible by foot from either end. Parking, however, is only available at the Pensacola Beach end. There is no charge to fish but non-residents require a fishing license.

⑭   Santa Rosa Island segment of the Gulf Islands National Seashore. Charge is the same as at Ft. Pickens. Good shore fishing and access to flats for wade fishing in Santa Rosa Sound. One particularly good flats area is around Big Sabine Point. No side-of-the-road parking is allowed, but four off-road parking areas with dune crossovers are spaced equidistantly along the park's seven mile length.

⑮   "Power lines" cross the East Bay River where it turns due east coming up from East Bay. Pilings are real fish attractors.

⑯   Navarre Bridge area including grass flats just East of the bridge.

Surf

Pensacola surf fishing opportunities are excellent along the entire 35 miles or so of accessible beach in the area. Despite the ravages of Hurricanes Erin and Opal in 1995, the bottom contour of this stretch of beach is basically the same. The beach slopes down to a trough which more or less parallels the shore. The first of two sandbars is on the far side of the trough, and it, too, parallels the beach. A second trough is on the far side of the first sandbar and a second sandbar is on the far side of that one. The flat sandy bottom of the Gulf begins beyond the second bar.

Cuts in bars, perpendicular to the beach, are also present and can be identified in two ways. The first is to look for darker colored water extending out into the Gulf across the bars. The second, if there are waves breaking, is to look for spots where they don't break, indicating the absence of the bar. Cuts occur randomly along the beach and provide a way for fish to come into the troughs along the beach to feed. All of these features are relatively easy to see from the beach due to the differences in water color.

From a surf fishing standpoint, bottom contour is fundamentally important because it tells you where to fish. The name of the game in the Pensacola area is to fish the cuts and troughs. Although there may be times during higher tides when fish chase bait across bars, the majority of the time they'll use the cuts to come in to feed in the relatively deeper waters of the troughs.

In addition to the Surf fish identified in the Species/Location Correlation Matrix presented in Chapter 1, non-edible species also frequent the Pensacola area surf and provide excellent sport. Those include a variety of Jacks, Saltwater Catfish, Sharks and Stingrays. And, there's always a chance for surprise-- like the isolated Cobia or King Mackerel that is caught now and then in the surf!

When to fish is an easy question to address for the Pensacola area surf because the answer is clear-cut. Although something may bite throughout the day (and night), all fish seem to bite best at three specific times. The first is at sunup, regardless of what the tide is doing. The second is around sundown, also regardless of the tide. The third is during the two hour period that precedes the high tide. If you have to choose only one of these three periods to fish, sunup is absolutely the best.

A few words about wind and its effects on the surf may also be helpful. Generally, Southeast, South and Southwest winds of up to 10-15 mph are good. They make waves in the Gulf. As these waves break over the bars, they churn up the sand and release the food that it holds--like sand fleas, crabs, etc. Hungry fish aren't far behind. Winds from any Northerly heading, however, do just the opposite. They generally stifle any wave action along the beach. As a result, food is not exposed and any fish in the area are not motivated to feed. The effects of winds from the East and West are really problematical. Sometimes fishing results are good-- and sometimes they're not. If in doubt, you can't tell without throwing in a line.

Now, specifics...starting at the Alabama line and moving East, points of interest are highlighted in the following figure. Explanations follow the maps.

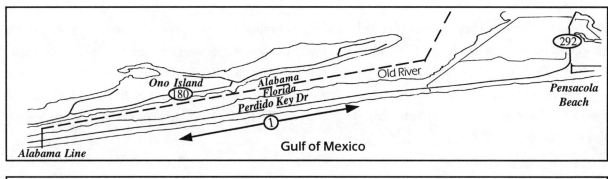

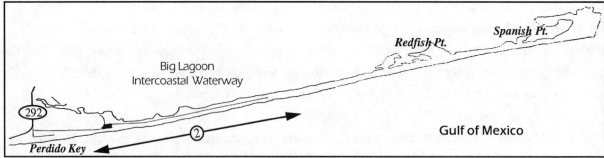

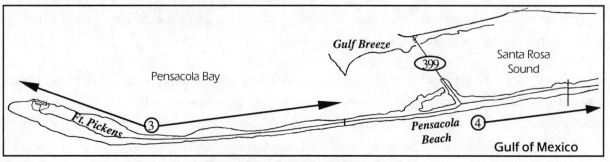

Figure 2.4 - **Pensacola Area Surf**

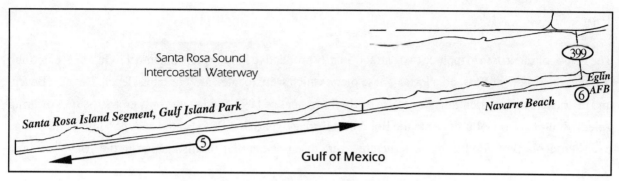

Figure 2.4 - **Pensacola Area Surf- (continued)**

Legend

① Perdido Key State Recreation Area - There is a total of 247 acres of prime, on-the-Gulf, surf fishing water within this state park, which is located just a couple of miles East of the Alabama line. Off road parking and nice facilities are available for a nominal charge. There is also relatively easy access to other surf spots on either side of the park despite existing development. The Florida portion of Perdido Key can also be good surf fishing, with Side-of-the-road parking and only a reasonable hike are required to fish these spots.

② Perdido Key Area - Gulf Islands National Seashore/Johnson Beach. The park is about two miles long. Perdido Key extends another five miles beyond the developed portion of the park. Access to that portion is strictly by foot but overnight camping is permitted. Excellent surf fishing along the entire seven miles. That is equally true of the flats wade fishing on Intercoastal Waterway side of the park. Park entrance fee is $4.00 per car and is good for seven days.

③ Ft. Pickens segment of the Gulf Islands National Seashore - Excellent, newly reconstructed facilities (post hurricanes Erin and Opal). Entrance fee is $4.00 per car and is good for seven days. Off road parking in several spots. Surf fishing superb, particularly along the beach adjacent to and around the jetties of Pensacola Pass. Camp sites available. A real year-round fishing location.

④ The best surf fishing about 500 yards East of the former Pensacola Beach pier. The bar and trough sturcture is relatively uniform and there are a couple of easily accesssible cuts in the bars.

⑤ Santa Rosa Island segment of the Gulf Islands National Seashore - More than five miles of potentially productive surf. A day use facility with off-road parking mid-way down this segment of Santa Rosa Island.

⑥ Navarre Beach Pier - Although the pier is partially destroyed and is now closed, the water around the remaining structure still provides outstanding fishing opportunities. Water around all but the end of the remaining pier is reachable by the surf fisherman casting from the beach.

Piers

The Pensacola area used to include two extraordinarily productive fishing piers out into the Gulf of Mexico and one into the waters of Pensacola Pass. These piers, which were located at Pensacola Beach, Navarre Beach, and Ft. Pickens, were essentially destroyed by the hurricanes of 1995. Today, the only area structures offering "pier fishing like" opportunities are the Bob Sikes Bridge over Santa Rosa Sound and the Three Mile Bridge over Pensacola Bay. Both of these structures were discussed earlier in this chapter in the "Bays" section.

Inshore

For our discussion purposes here, we've defined Pensacola Inshore waters as extending out about five miles from the beach from the Alabama line to Navarre Beach. The following spots, which include both natural and artificial bottom structure, are located in these waters.

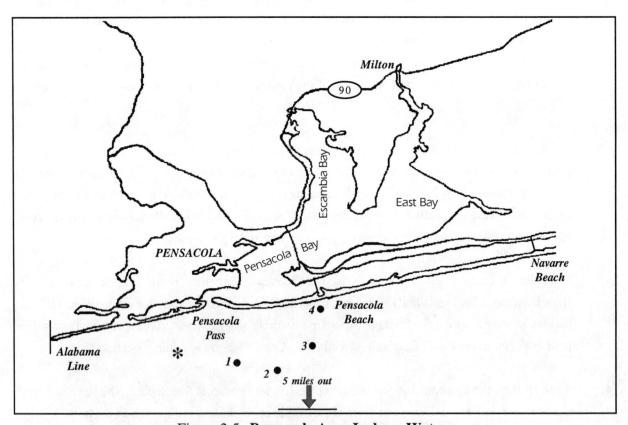

Figure 2.5 - **Pensacola Area Inshore Waters**

If you're going to head out for some Pensacola area Inshore trolling, you need to be ready to fish as soon as you enter the Pass. At various times of the year, the Pass itself and for about a mile around its mouth are choice areas for King and Spanish Mackerel, Cobia, Redfish, Blackfin Tuna and occasionally Tarpon. You'll want to check the immediate areas around the channel markers for sure. You can usually catch your live bait on these markers too.

The listing of Inshore fishing spots that follows is designed for use by LORAN equipped boats. The LORAN coordinates are uncorrected for plotting on navigational charts. Also, and due to the varying approach of local artificial reef programs on reporting location by LORAN coordinates, there can be no guarantee that the numbers provided correspond to the center of deployed material. If, when trying to locate an artificial reef, your depth finder does not indicate material on the bottom, start a circular search pattern and gradually expand it until material is located.

Spot #	Name	LORAN Coordinates	Depth (ft)	Structure
1	Three Barges	13270.6/47107.6	54	Coal barges, concrete rubble
2	Liberty Ship Reef	13306.8/47102.5	82	Libery Ship "J. L. Meek"
3	Casino Fishing Reef	13333.3/47115.0	60	Concrete rubble
4	Pensacola Beach Pier	N/A	40-60	Remains of the former pier

Figure 2.6 - **Inshore Spot Location Coordinates**

In addition to the numbered spots shown in Figure 2.5, one other location is indicated with an asterisk. It is by far the most interesting of all. The asterisk indicates the final resting spot of the oldest existing American battleship, the USS Massachusetts. Officially commissioned by the Navy on June 10, 1896, she was over 350 feet long, with a beam of 69 feet and a draft of 24 feet. Today, the remains of the USS Massachusetts are in 26 feet of water a mile and a half South - Southwest of Pensacola Pass. The site is easily located because the ship's two main gun turrets are awash most of the time. The wreck is also marked by a red bell buoy shown on the charts as WR2. Applicable LORAN numbers are: 13215.0/47108.9.

Two other spots slightly farther offshore may be of interest to you. The first is a 1/10 square mile of bridge rubble located in 80 feet of water, LORAN: 13278.0/47091.8. The second is a barge sunk in 75 feet of water, LORAN: 13306.9/47102.8.

The majority of the time, the entire area covered by the map can be easily and safely fished in a relatively small boat. In stormy or excessively windy weather, however, just getting out through the mouth of Pensacola Pass can be harrowing, if not plain dangerous. Before heading out the Pass, and as a minimum, always check for small craft advisories and whether or not the charter boat fleet has gone out. If it hasn't, you know the Gulf is no place for a small boat that day.

As a final but fundamentally obvious note, while fishing Inshore, keep your eyes on the charter boats. The professionals that run these boats have the experience and sophisticated electronics to always find the fish. Watch them, emulate what they do, and stay with them. But, and most importantly, don't get in their way while they're making their living. In this regard, when you see a group of charter boats working a particular area, DO NOT head for the middle of them. Lay back and look for the pattern of movement. More often than not, they will be following each other in some sort of a circle. If this is the case, start your own circle just outside theirs. You'll catch plenty of fish -- while not provoking an incident at sea.

Offshore

As noted earlier in this chapter, the Pensacola, Destin, and Panama City areas all share the same superb Desoto Canyon waters for world class big game fishing. Because of this, and to minimize unnecessary redundancy, these waters will only be described once, here, in the Pensacola section. However, appropriate cross references will be provided in both the Destin and Panama City area sections later in this chapter.

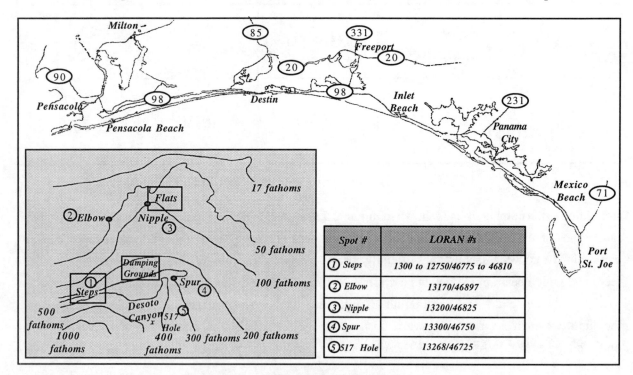

Figure 2.7 - **Offshore Desoto Canyon Area**

The map of the Offshore Desoto Canyon area highlights potentially productive structure and significant features in Offshore waters. If billfish are your bag, a good spot to start trolling is at the Nipple. It's where a fisherman will first find 100 fathom waters and is some 30 nautical miles SSE of Pensacola Pass. The Nipple annually produces good numbers of White Marlin and Wahoo. Big Blue Marlin, however, are another hour's run due South. Look for them beyond the 400 fathom line, with smaller rats inside the 100 fathom curve.

Another pattern for far Offshore trolling is to fish the Loop Current that parallels the coast some 60-100 miles out. Since the water temperature remains constant in this current year round, the Loop is a good place to work during late summer when the water closer in becomes excessively hot. Obviously, a good thermometer is critical to finding and staying in the cooler water of the Loop Current.

The 29 fathom curve, known as the "Edge", offers good combination fishing. If trolling doesn't produce, watch your depth recorder, find a spike, break out the bottom fishing tackle, and have at it. While you're doing that, you might also want to drift a live or fresh dead bait for any pelagic species that may wander by. Closer in, the key to big bull Dolphin and Wahoo can often be weed lines as close as 10 miles from shore.

Offshore bottom fishing off Pensacola can be outstanding every month of the year. Productive spots comprised of either natural or artificial bottom structure are readily accessible to area fishermen. Several of the more popular man-made sites are highlighted below. Adjacent Destin area bottom fishing spots may also be of interest.

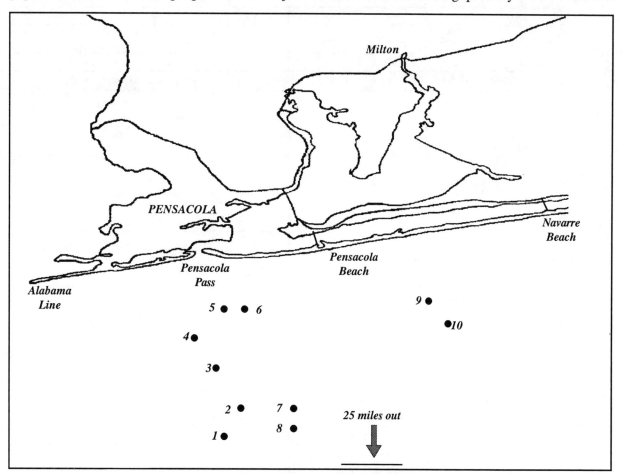

Figure 2.8 - **Offshore Fishing Spots**

As with the Inshore table in the previous section, Offshore spot location data is designed for use by LORAN equipped boats. The caveats presented relative to given LORAN coordinates are equally applicable here. Although not shown in the Figure 2.9, one additional set of LORAN coordinates is worthy of mention: 13546.7/ 47063.3. These are the coordinates of a very old tug boat called the Zeus that was recently sunk some 18 miles Southwest of Destin.

Spot#	Site Name	LORAN Coordinates	Depth (ft.)	Structure
1	Miss Jenny 20-3	13248.8/47006.5	115	53' steel supply boat
	The Silos	13250.3-4/47005.5	124	Tanks, plastic containers, culverts
	The Silos	13248.9/47004.4	117	Tanks, plastic containers, culverts
2	San Pablo	13263.8/47077.1	84	Navy Target Ship
3	ARCOA Reef	13251.5/47068.8	89	30 Prefab PVC pipe modules
	CSX Rubble 7-QQ#2	13255.1/47065.8	90	Small concrete bridge span
	CSX Rubble 7-QQ#4	13255.5/47065.6	90	10' Concrete bridge section
	Steel Scrap 7-J	13248.0/47062.4	91	Steel scrap structures, 10 cars each
	Culverts 7-JJ	13254.7/47069.2	87	Concrete culverts
	Steel Scrap 7-G	13247.5/47068.1	78	Scrap steel structures, 10 cars each
	Tug Philip 7-ZZ	13256.2/47059.4	95	60' Steel tugboat 'Philip'
	CSX Rubble 7-QQ#3	13255.5/47065.7	90	10' Concrete bridge section
	Culverts 7-L	13248.7/47068.9	81	150 concrete culverts
	Tug, FAA Pipes 7-K	13247.6/47060.8	95	65' Tug 'Born Again' 21 stanchion pipes
	CSX Rubble 7-QQ#1	13255.1/47065.9	90	8' Concrete bridge section
	CSX Rubble 7-QQ#5	13255.7/47065.6	90	Large concrete bridge span
	CSX Rubble barge 7-QQ	13255.6/47065.6	90	Concrete, barge pieces
	LCM 7-11	13253.0/47060.6	91	56' LCM Steel vessel
	Tugboat Heron 7-11	13253.0/47060.6	91	53' Tugboat 'Heron'
4	Monsanto Boxes 15-T	13247.7/47079.7	69	Cluster of steel modules
	FAA Tower 15-V	13253.6/47076.3	75	3 modules of radio tower sections
	ECUA Culverts 15-C	13252.0/47082.0	81	Concrete Culverts
	Monsanto Boxes 15-S	13248.7/47081.3	67	Steel Modules
	Scrap Steel 15-J	13254.3/47082.8	66	Scrap steel 10 car bodies
	Pipe Ends 15-PE FRB	13247.6/47076.5	77	10 car bodies
	Tessie 15-PE FRB	13250.1/47078.4	75	Steel water tower pipe ends, near 'Tessie'
	Culverts 15-PE FRB	13250.0/4707.5	75	100 concrete culverts surround 'Tessie' hull
	Tugboat Sylvia 15-W	13247.7/47074.7	79	65' Steel tugboat 'Deliverance'
	Scrap Steel	13252.5/47075.5	82	48' Tugboat 'Sylvia'
	PC Barge 15-V	13247.0/47081.6	65	Steel scrap 10 car bodies
		13253.6/47076.3	75	110' steel barge
5	Bridge Rubble	13278.0/47091.8	80	Concrete Rubble 1/10 sq. mi.
6	1982 Barge	13306.9/47102.8	75	Barge
7	Jones Reef	13330.0/47020.0	150	Unknown
8	McKay Reef	13348.2/47028.0	156	Tires, appliances, shopping carts
	Tenneco Reef	13324.5/47012.7	156	Dismantled oil platform
	Woodburn Reef	13300.4/47010.1	138	Truck cabs
9	Barnes Site 6	13500.0/47090.0	-	Unknown
10	Liberty Ship Reef	13515.2/47083.9	85	440' Liberty ship "Joseph E. Brown"

Figure 2.9 - **Offshore Spot Location Coordinates**

Several other spots may also be of interest to you. The first is a former natural gas platform emplaced a couple of years ago. The platform, located on the bottom 18.5 miles off Pensacola, is in two pieces. The LORAN coordinates for the larger piece are 13361.9/47037.2. It rests in 135 feet of water and rises 77 feet off the bottom. The second piece is 50 feet to the West and rises 40 feet off the bottom.

Thirteen sunken Army M-60 tanks represent another possibility for good bottom fishing. The LORAN numbers are provided below:

• Tank #1	13247.00	47068.70		• Tank #8	13247.00	47066.60
• Tank #2	13247.40	47068.40		• Tank #9	13268.10	47052.20
• Tank #3	13247.40	47068.10		• Tank #10	13268.30	47052.30
• Tank #4	13247.30	47067.70		• Tank #11	13268.50	47052.30
• Tank #5	13248.00	47066.80		• Tank #12	13268.70	47052.30
• Tank #6	13248.50	47066.60		• Tank #13	13268.60	47052.60
• Tank #7	13247.40	47065.60				

The Pete Tide 2 is another spot you might want to check. This 180 foot former oil field supply ship is in 104 feet of water 11.8 nautical miles South-Southeast of the Pass. LORAN numbers are: 13250.5/47063.6.

So, that's the top and bottom of the Desoto Canyon and Offshore bottom fishing story. The Desoto Canyon is an extraordinary area that, in at least in one respect, is unique. In 1972, for the first time ever recorded, a *Panhandle* area fisherman accomplished a Super Grand Slam. On an overnight trip, he successfully landed a Blue Marlin, White Marlin, Sailfish, and a Swordfish. Although few anglers try for Grand Slams (a Super Grand without the Swordfish) or Super Grand Slams these days, the Desoto Canyon area is one of the few places in the world where it's possible.

OK, so much for the Pensacola area. It truly does have something for everyone. But, the fish are biting to the East too. We need to move along -- to the Destin area -- and get ready to **CATCH FISH NOW!**

DESTIN AREA

The Destin area , for our purposes here, lies between Navarre Beach and Inlet Beach. Like the Pensacola area, it too offers superior opportunities for Bay, Surf, Pier, Inshore, and Offshore fishing. As you can see below, the 33 mile long Choctawhatchee Bay is a prominent feature of the area. The bay is fed by the Choctawhatchee River system on its East end and Destin's East Pass at the West end. Santa Rosa Sound also feeds into the bay on its West end. Over 20 bayous open onto the bay and offer great fishing almost year round. In addition to the bay, adjacent bayous, and Santa Rosa Sound, the Destin area also offers over 50 miles of fishable surf, a fishing pier on Okaloosa Island, and excellent Inshore trolling and bottom fishing opportunities. An abundance of Offshore artificial and natural bottom structure provides similar good opportunities to catch deep water bottom dwellers. And, as noted earlier, Destin shares and has good access to the fertile big game waters of the Desoto Canyon area.

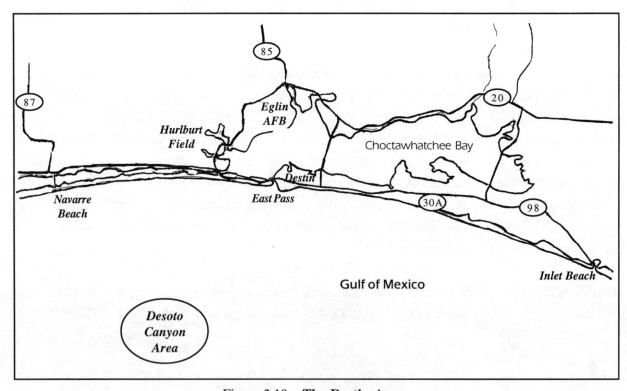

Figure 2.10 - **The Destin Area**

Figure 2.11, the fishing activity summary, reflects the same kind of catch data as presented in Chapter 1. In this case, however, only Destin area activity is highlighted.

As Figure 2.11 reflects, something's biting in Destin area waters every month of the year. Although the monthly fishing activity data has necessarily been generalized, it does provide useful insights into when you can reasonably expect to catch a particular kind of fish--or what kind of fish you can expect to catch in any given month. For example, in any given year, you can generally expect to catch Redfish somewhere in the Destin area every month of the year. King Mackerel, on the other hand, usually only show up during the months of

Panhandle Gamefish	Historic Monthly Activity											
	J	F	M	A	M	J	J	A	S	O	N	D
Amberjack	X	X	X	X	XXX	XX	XXX	XXX	XXX	XX	X	X
Black Drum	X	XX	XX	XX	X	XXX	X	XX	XX	X	XX	XX
Black Sea Bass												
Blackfin Tuna			X	X	X	XX	XX	X	XX	XX	X	
Bluefish	X	X	X	X	XX	XX	XX	XX	X	X	X	X
Blue Marlin					X	XX	XX	X	XX	X	X	
Bonito	X			X	XX	XX	XXX	XXX	XX	XX	X	
Cobia			X	XXX	XXX	XX	X	X	X	X		
Dolphin				X	XX	XX	XXX	XX	XXX	X	X	
Flounder	X	X	X	XX	XX	XX	X	XX	XXX	XX	XXX	XXX
Grouper	X	X	XX	XX	XX	X	XX	XX	XX	XX	X	X
Jack Cravalle			X	X	XX	X	X	XXX	XX	X	X	
King Mackerel				X	XX	XXX	XXX	XXX	XX	XX	X	
Northern Mackerel	X		X	XX	XX	XXX	XX	X	X	X	X	
Pompano		X	X	XXX	XXX	XX	X	X	X	X		
Redfish	X	X	XX	XX	XXX	XXX	XX	XXX	XX	XX	XX	X
Sailfish						X	X	XX	XX	X	X	
Sheepshead	XX	XX	XX	XXX	XXX	XX	XXX	XX	XX	XX	XX	XXX
Snapper	X	X	XX	XX	XX	XX	XX	XX	XX	XX	XX	X
Spanish Mackerel		X	X	XXX	XXX	XXX	XXX	XX	XX	XX	X	
Swordfish								X				
Tarpon					X	XX	XXX	XX				
Triggerfish	X	X	XX	XX	XXX	XX	XX	XX	XX	XX	XX	X
Tripletail												
Trout	X	X	XX	XX	XXX	XX	XX	X	XX	XX	X	X
Wahoo					X	XX	XX	XX	X	X	X	
White Marlin						X	XX	XX	X	X		
Whiting			X	X	XX	XXX	XXX	XX	XX	X	X	
Yellowfin Tuna						X	XX	XX	X	X		

Legend: Blank= No reported activity   XX= Good catches reported during the month

X= At least a few reported caught in the area during the month   XXX= Great. Even if you just do a few things right, you're going to catch fish

Figure 2.11 - **Destin Area Annual Fishing Summary**

April through November. The following narrative sharpens up the generalized focus of Figure 2.11. It describes area fishing activity on a month-by-month basis using specific catch data obtained from area tackle stores, landings, etc. The locations identified in the data will be highlighted in the maps and charts that follow.

January

- Specs, Reds, Sheepshead and Red Snapper on the "Old Ship" in Choctawhatchee Bay.
- Grouper, Snapper, Triggerfish and Amberjacks (AJ's) in 60-100 feet of water Offshore.
- Pompano off the Okaloosa Island Pier.
- Specs in canals adjacent to Santa Rosa Sound.
- Sheepshead, Reds and Flounder around Brooks Bridge.
- Bull Reds and some Specs off the Highway 331 Bridge.

February

- Specs and Reds at the mouth of the Choctawhatchee River.
- Snapper and Grouper on Offshore structure in 150-300 feet of water.
- Sheepshead on all bay bridges (Destin, Brooks, Cinco, Shalimar, Mid-Bay and Highway 331).

March

- Cobia starting to show along the beach.
- Gag Grouper Offshore in 180 feet of water.
- Red and Black Snapper on wrecks and reefs in 50-90 feet of water.
- Pompano beginning to show in the surf.
- Bull Reds at the Destin Bridge.
- Pompano, Sheepshead, Black Drum and Bluefish at East Pass jetties.
- Best bottom fishing Offshore at the "Edge" in 200+ feet of water. Big AJ's.
- Specs biting well in Hogtown Bayou.
- Sheepshead and Black Drum on all bay bridges.
- Spanish Mackerel starting to show at the East Pass jetties and Inshore off the beach.
- Cobia, Pompano, Sheepshead, Spanish and Reds off the pier.

April

- Cobia from the outer bar to one-half mile off the beach.
- Pompano in the surf.
- Flounder starting to show around bay and bayou structure.
- Spanish Mackerel widely scattered in the bay.
- Cobia, Spanish, Pompano, Sheepshead, Black Drum, Bonito and Northern Mackerel off the pier.
- King Mackerel starting to show Inshore.
- Specs and Reds on the Choctawhatchee River delta.
- Big Specs in the mouths of Mack and Hewitt Bayous.
- Offshore bottom fishing excellent.

May

- Specs spreading out on all grass flats.
- Kings over Inshore structure.
- Spanish, Pompano, Reds, Flounder, Sheepshead and Black Drum off the East Pass jetties.
- Wahoo and Dolphin starting to show Offshore.

June

- Kings widely scattered Inshore.
- Tarpon at the "Old Ship" in Choctawhatchee Bay (First full moon).
- Blue and White Marlin, bull and schoolie Dolphin and Yellowfin Tuna starting to show Offshore.
- Wahoo are also cooperating as close as 6-7 miles out.
- Schoolie Dolphin available Inshore at the "Bridge Rubble".
- Ladyfish (Poor Man's Tarpon) in the sound and bayous.
- Reds, Specs, Sheepshead and Flounder widely scattered in the bay, bayous and sound.

July

- Specs and Reds remain on the flats.
- Pompano continue in the surf, off the pier and at the jetties.
- Specs heavy in the bay at White Point.
- Schoolie Dolphin along Inshore weedlines.
- Grouper, Snapper and Triggers in less than 100 feet of water.
- Jack Cravalle roaming Inshore/Bay waters.
- Kings and Spanish widely scattered Inshore. Big Kings in the Timberhole area.
- White Marlin, Wahoo and Blackfin Tuna around the "Nipple" and out toward the "Spur".
- Tarpon along the beach off Sandestin.

August

- World Class Jack Cravalle terrorizing the bay and bayous.
- Blue and White Marlin, Sailfish, Blackfin and Yellowfin Tuna and Wahoo in Desoto Canyon area. Swordfish at night in the same area.
- Reds, Specs, Flounder, Sheepshead and Black Drum widely scattered in the bay, bayous and sound around all bridges.
- Kings and Spanish still Inshore.

September

- Jack Cravalle to 40+ pounds in the bay.
- Trolling and bottom fishing for all species excellent Offshore.
- Blackfin Tuna Inshore.
- Specs on bay grass flats early and late.
- Kings active over Inshore structure.
- Several legal Cobia caught in area bayous.
- Tarpon off the pier.
- Tarpon and various kinds of Sharks in the East end of the bay.

October

- AJ's, Grouper, Snapper and Triggers good on Offshore structure.
- Kings and Spanish remain Inshore.
- Reds, Specs and Flounder widely scattered in the bay, bayous and sound.
- Grouper and Red Snapper on structure in less than 100 feet of water.

November

- Grouper, Snapper, AJ's and Triggers on Offshore structure.
- Red and Black Snapper Inshore on structure in 30-70 feet of water.
- Flounder on Inshore structure off East Pass.
- Bonito, Whiting, Reds, Flounder, Pompano and small Grouper off the pier.
- Bluefish off the Destin Coast Guard Station.
- Reds in the surf.
- Specs and Reds in Four Mile and Alaqua Creeks.
- Kings and Blackfin Tuna Inshore and off the pier.
- Specs moving off flats into deeper water and towards the heads of bayous.
- Spanish in some bayous.
- Legal Grouper in the bay in the deepest holes and off the Shalimar and Mid-Bay bridges.
- Reds, Flounder, smallish Grouper and Bluefish off the jetties.
- Black Drum, Reds, Black Sea Bass, Black Snapper and Flounder on the Mid-bay Bridge.

December

- Grouper, Snapper, Triggers and AJ's Offshore in 100 feet of water.
- Flounder spawning at the mouth of East Pass.
- Specs at the heads of most bayous and in creeks feeding into the bay.
- Specs and Reds upstream in the Choctawhatchee River system.
- Flounder in the Surf.
- Whiting, Flounder, Sheepshead, Reds and Bonito off the pier.
- Bluefish widely scattered in the bay.

Bays

Fishing in Choctawhatchee Bay, its bayous and Santa Rosa Sound west to Navarre Beach can be productive for one or more good eating fish almost year round. For a variety of reasons, however, Choctawhatchee Bay and surrounding waters have not been fished intensively. As a result, they continue to possess an as yet untapped potential for truly outstanding sport fishing.

Due to its size, fishing opportunities in the Bay are widely dispersed. Accordingly, coverage of the area will be presented in smaller geographical pieces that can each be fished in a single day. These pieces include:

- *West end of the Bay*, adjacent bayous and Santa Rosa Sound west to Navarre Beach
- *East end of the Bay* from the Mid-Bay Bridge to the Choctawhatchee River delta

Maps of each of these areas follow. Each will be numerically annotated to indicate points or places that may be of interest to you. Descriptive comments are provided for each map.

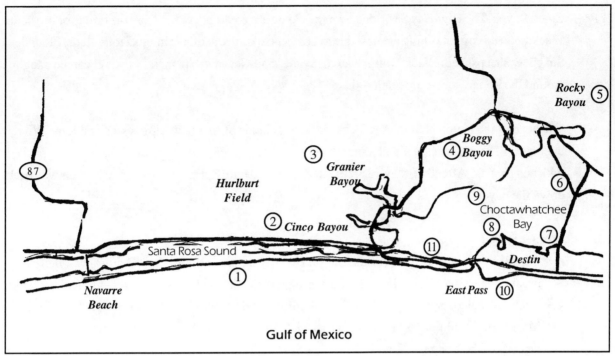

Figure 2.12A - **West End - Choctawhatchee Bay**

Legend

①   Santa Rosa Sound (also a part of the Intercoastal Waterway). Moving from West to East, specific points of interest include the following:

- Navarre Bridge. Good area to fish for almost all area species year round.

- Hurlburt Field. The Air Force has a Rec Services/boat ramp/marina operation on the Sound. There are a number of good spots to fish in the immediate area, including the deep water around the fuel docks. Trout, Redfish and Flounder are always possibilities.

- Old deep water residential docks on the North side of the channel. Can be fished productively by either casting lures around dock pilings or, if the wind is right, drifting with live bait.

- Liza Jackson Park. Nice facilities, good boat ramp and restrooms. Easy access for wade fishermen.

- Deep water around some of the dock/slips belonging to the condos and other commercial facilities on shore. Flylining large live bait often produces large Trout and Reds.

- Aquatic Enterprises. South side of the Sound on the West side of Brooks Bridge. A full-service bait and tackle shop right on the water. Food, fuel and outstanding information on how to fish Santa Rosa Sound are always available. Also very knowledgeable about other kinds of fishing in the area.

- Brooks Bridge. The waters around the bridge routinely produce great fishing for all kinds of fish usually caught in the bay. Sometimes even the unusual, like Cobia, wander by.

- Grass Flats. On the North side where the Sound meets the bay, this relatively shallow area (3-6 feet) often provides great wade fishing, with Trout one of the primary targets. Shore access is possible from several streets that dead-end at the Sound.

②   Cinco Bayou. The Highway 85 bridge over the bayou is a great spot either from the bridge or in a boat. Weekdays and early morning are best due to heavy boat traffic at other times. Trout, Reds, Flounder, Snapper, Sheepshead, Black Drum, Jack Cravalle, Sail Cats and Spanish Mackerel can be caught around the bridge at one time or another.

    The head of the bayou is of interest because several kinds of fish including Specs and Reds Winter over here. There is usually about a month period in the late Fall when the area is absolutely packed with hungry fish. After that, they're pretty much dormant until Spring when they make their way back down the bayou.

③   Garnier Bayou
   - The Highway 85 bridge over the bayou (locally called the Shalimar Bridge) can be fished productively either from a boat or off the bridge. Good fishing for something year round. Possible catch can include Specs and White Trout, Reds, Flounder, Jack Cravalle, Sheepshead, and Spanish Mackerel. In addition, some truly huge Black Drum (70+ pounds) as well as legal Cobia have been landed off the bridge.
   - Creeks entering the headwaters of the bayou are excellent places for Reds in the late Fall.
   - Deep water holes off the old Hudson's Marina frequently hold large Specs and Reds during the hottest part of the summer.
   - The flats and holes around the county maintenance yard at the mouth of the bayou are collectively a good area to fish early and late in the day (flats) and during mid-day (holes). In the Spring and early Summer, noisy top water plugs like Zara Spooks fished after dark can produce big Specs.

④   Boggy Bayou. There are several nice public parks on the bayou, one on either side, with good facilities and boat ramps.
   - Niceville Fishermen's Co-op. Commercial fishing boats regularly off-load at the Co-op. Perhaps there's some spillage in the process. In any event, there are always large fish resident in the deep water behind the Co-op. Live Pinfish are the bait of choice.
   - Interesting spot. Almost to the head of the bayou, on the East side, is a townhome complex. Just to the right of it, a small creek enters the bayou. The area around the mouth of the creek routinely holds nice Specs and Flounder--and Largemouth Bass.

⑤   Rocky Bayou. The Highway 20 bridge over the bayou is a great spot for Specs, Reds, Snapper and Jacks. A boat is required. Work the West side of the bridge almost exclusively since the remnants of an old bridge are on the bottom. The Fred Gannon Rocky Bayou State Park is on the South side of the bayou. Nice place for a family outing, good place for the kids to fish and crab, and big Specs roam the shallows early in the morning.

⑥   Grass Flats. There are extensive grass flats along this entire stretch in five to eight feet of water. In the Spring and Fall, this is a productive area for Specs and Reds--on either conventional tackle or fly fishing. In the Summer, early morning and sundown top water fishing for Specs is usually successful. The Specs seem to move around, so the name of the game is troll till you find them. Then, stop and cast.

⑦ Indian Bayou. Good for Reds, Specs, Flounder, Sheepshead, and Black Drum. Boat required since surface access is tough.

⑧ Joe's Bayou. Lots of deep water so productive for one or more of the following year round: Specs; Reds; Snapper; Sheepshead; and, Black Drum.

⑨ Choctawatchee Bay Artificial Reef. This reef, installed in 1987, consists of 12 polyolefin cones submerged in 26 feet of water. The cones provide a relief of 12 feet. LORAN coordinates for the reef are: 13733.1 and 47158.4. Red Snapper to 26 pounds and sizable grouper have come from spots like this in Choctawatchee Bay. But, don't forget the caveat on LORAN numbers presented earlier. The cones may not be where they were originally implaced. So, keep your bottom machine on and look around.

⑩ East Pass. Although all the fish in the Pass move around some, there are basic patterns to their location and preferred habitats. With the exception of the Reds, all of the species noted below seem to be either unaffected by tidal action or more active on an incoming tide. Traditionally, the Redfish seem to bite better on an outgoing tide.
- Black Drum - Along the channel sides of both jetties and around the deep water bridge pilings.
- Bluefish - Off the jetties and around the Coast Guard Station.
- Flounder - The best spots have consistently been in the turbulent water of the East side and tip of the East jetty. They are also caught along the edges of the channel and around the docks in Destin Harbor.
- Jack Cravalle - From time to time, large schools have frequented Destin harbor, the bridge pilings, and around the Coast Guard Station.
- Northern Mackerel - Off the jetties.
- Pompano - East side and tip of the East jetty.
- Redfish - The area around the bridge pilings on the East side of the Pass and along the channel sides of both jetties.
- Sheepshead - Around bridge and dock pilings throughout the area.
- Snapper - Around the bridge.
- Specs - Destin harbor, Sandpiper Cove, and the canals on Holiday Isle. The area around the jetty at the Coast Guard Station has also been very productive.

⑪ Okaloosa Island. Although an island in name only, this sliver of predominantly Air Force land extends from Destin's East Pass to just past Brooks Bridge over Santa Rosa Sound. On its bay side, the island offers several good areas to fish. They're identified below, starting at the Coast Guard Station on the

East end of the island.

- Coast Guard Station. There are always some kind of fish active off the station's jetty year 'round. Adjacent waters typically hold Specs, Bluefish, some Reds, Jack Cravalle, Flounder, and Spanish Mackerel. Active duty military are frequently permitted to fish from the jetty.
- Flats. These flats basically run along the North side of the channel from the Coast Guard Station West about two miles. The entire stretch can be productive early in the morning and in the early evening. After the hurricanes of 1995; it is a long wade out to good water.
- Gulf Islands National Seashore Park. Good access for wade fishing on surrounding flats and the Intercoastal Waterway channel.
- Ross Marler Park. Public boat ramp and good fishing out into the deeper waters of the Intercoastal Waterway. Turn into the park off Santa Rosa Blvd.

Figure 2.12B highlights the East end of the Bay, which starts at the Mid-Bay Bridge and extends some 20 miles to the East.

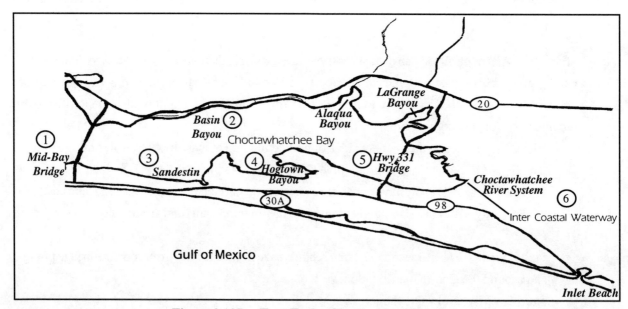

Figure 2.12B - **East End - Choctawhatchee Bay**

Legend

①   Mid-Bay Bridge. In a very short period of time, this new bridge has become a significant "fish attraction device" in the Choctawhatchee Bay. All bay species can routinely be caught around the bridge support structures. Legal Grouper are a distinct possibility too.

②   Basin Bayou. About one mile South and a little West of this bayou, there's a sunken ship. It's called the "old ship" by the local folks. The wreck is in 20 feet of water and has structure that extends above the surface. Gator Specs to 8-9 pounds, Jack Cravalle up to 40 pounds, and substantially sized Tarpon are good Summer possibilities. Tarpon usually show up on the first full moon in June.

③   Sandestin. The waters around this resort community are excellent fishing. Horseshoe Bayou is a part of the Sandestin complex and contains the resort's Baytowne Marina. Rental boats are available. Specs, Reds, Flounder, and from time to time, Jack Cravalle can be caught in the bayou and the channel leading into it. On the East side of the Sandestin promontory that juts out into the Bay (Four Mile Point), there are three relatively small bayous: Buck; Mack; and, Hewitt. All three are good for Reds and Specs. Shore fishing in Mack Bayou is possible off Mack Bayou Road and in Hewitt Bayou off Hewitt Road.

④   Hogtown Bayou. In addition to excellent fishing for Specs and Reds, the head of this bayou offers very large Flounder in the late Summer and early Fall period. There is a boat ramp off State Road 393.

⑤   Highway 331 Bridge. Superior fishing for all bay species most of the year. The 331 Bait and Tackle Shop on the highway close to the north end of the causeway is a good source for current fishing information. Actual fishing areas are sections of the previous causeway and 331 bridge that are now accessible from the new causeway. There are also small boat launch ramps along the new causeway.

⑥   Choctawhatchee River System. From Freeport, go South on Highway 331 a couple of miles and follow signs East to Black Creek Lodge. Boat ramp provides access to Choctawhatchee River delta. Multiple river mouths. Year round opportunities for Reds, Specs and Sheepshead. Sunshine (hybrid) Bass and Flounder are other possibilities. In the early Fall, big Reds and Specs roam the flats at the river mouths. Flat at the "South Mouth" considered by locals to be the best. South mouth is about a quarter mile south of the main mouth of the Choctawhatchee.

Surf

The entire 50 or so miles of fishable surf in the Destin area can be good fishing at any given time. Despite the ravages of Hurricanes Erin and Opal in 1995, the bottom contour of this stretch of beach remains basically the same as always. The beach slopes down to a trough which more or less parallels the shore. The first of two sandbars is on the far side of the trough, and it, too, parallels the beach. A second trough is on the far side of the first sandbar and a second sandbar is on the far side of that one. The flat sandy bottom of the Gulf begins beyond the second bar.

Cuts in bars, perpendicular to the beach, are also present and can be identified in two ways. The first is to look for darker colored water extending out into the Gulf across the bars. The second, if there are waves breaking, is to look for spots where they don't break, indicating an absence of the bar. Cuts occur randomly along the beach and provide a way for fish to come in to the troughs along the beach to feed. All of these features are relatively easy to see from the beach due to the differences in water color.

From a surf fishing standpoint, bottom contour is fundamentally important because it tells you where to fish. The name of the game in the Destin area is to fish the cuts and troughs. Although there may be times during higher tides when fish chase bait across bars, the majority of the time they'll use the cuts to come in to feed in the relatively deeper waters of the troughs.

\In addition to the surf fish identified in the Species/Location Correlation Matrix presented in Chapter 1, non-edible species also frequent the Destin area surf and provide excellent sport. Those include a variety of Jacks, Ladyfish, Sharks and Stingrays. And, there's always a chance for surprise--like the isolated Cobia or King Mackerel that is caught now and then in the surf!

When to fish is an easy question to address for the Destin area surf because the answer is clear-cut. Although something may bite throughout the day (and night), all fish seem to bite best at three specific times. The first is at sunup, regardless of what the tide is doing. The second is around sundown, also regardless of the tide. The third is during the two hour period that precedes the high tide. If you have to choose only one of these three periods to fish, sunup is absolutely the best.

A few words about wind and its effects on the surf may also be helpful. Generally, Southeast, South and Southwest winds of up to 10-15 mph are good. They make waves in the Gulf. As these waves break over the bars, they churn up the sand and release the food that it holds-- like sand fleas, crabs, etc. Hungry fish aren't far behind. Winds from any Northerly heading, however, do just the opposite. They generally stifle any wave action along the beach. As a result, food is not exposed and any fish in the area are not motivated to feed. The effects of winds from the East and west are really problematical. Sometimes fishing results are good-- and sometimes they're not. If in doubt, you can't tell without throwing a line out.

Starting at the Western end of development on Okaloosa Island and moving East, specific points of interest are highlighted on the following maps.

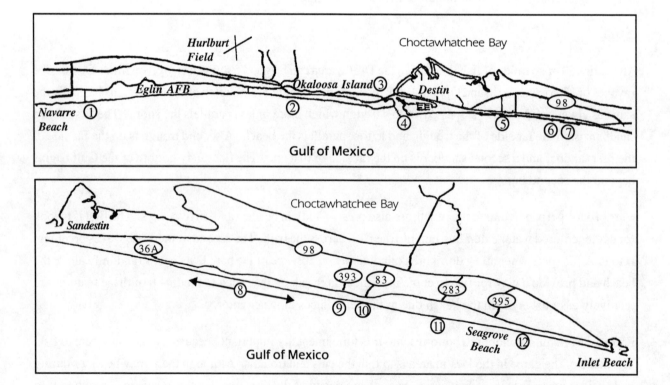

Figure 2.13 - **Destin Area Surf**

Legend

①   Public beach with off-road parking just East of the former Navarre Beach pier.

②   John Beasley Wayside Park. Located just East of the Okaloosa Island pier, the park offers the beach, picnic tables, barbecue grills, and rest rooms.

③   Okaloosa Island. Although the majority of the island is Air Force land, the public is not prohibited from walking across it or fishing on its beaches. You can park anywhere on the shoulder along Highway 98. Be careful of soft sand.

④   East Pass jetties. The surf to the East of the East jetty has been very good for Flounder and Pompano. It has also yielded good catches of Spanish Mackerel and Bluefish. Drive almost to the end of Gulf Shore Drive on Holiday Isle and park wherever you can. It's a pretty good hike to the beach from there. Fish early or late to avoid the crowds from adjacent condos.

⑤   Henderson Beach State Park. This relatively new park has great facilities and provides easy access for surf fisherman. The park's entrance is off Highway 98. Entrance fee is $3.25 per car.

⑥   Old Crystal Beach Pier. Although only a few pilings remain, there are several deep holes in the area that can be reached from the beach. Pompano, Bluefish, Reds, Flounder, and Spanish Mackerel are all possibilities. Access is problematic due to the condo density along this stretch of beach.

⑦   Crystal Beach Wayside Park. This county park has rest rooms, picnic tables, and parking with immediate access to the adjacent surf.

⑧   Highway 30A to Inlet Beach. There are still many undeveloped lots along the beach that provide ready access for surf fishermen. Road-side parking only.

⑨   Ed Wallins Park. On the water where County Road 393 meets Highway 30. Off road parking. A couple of nice cuts through the bars just East of the dune walkover.

⑩   Blue Mountain Beach Public Park. Off-road parking.

⑪   Grayton Beach State recreation Area. In addition to great surf fishing, this park also offers camping, boating and swimming on a fresh water lake, and other nature related activities.

⑫   Public Park. Going East on Highway 30A, turn off just East of Eastern Lake (Lakewood Dr).

Okaloosa Island Pier

The Okaloosa Island Pier is located just a mile or so east of Brooks Bridge and five miles west of the Destin Bridge on Highway 98. It's easy to find, since it has prominent neighbors--a large Ramada Inn complex to its East and the Gulfarium to its West. There is also a large PIER sign on the highway, adjacent to the parking access road. The pier itself used to extend some 1260 feet into the Gulf of Mexico. After the 1995 hurricanes, however, it's now about 500 feet in length. No saltwater fishing license is required. The pier operator has a blanket license which covers all fishermen. Cost to use the pier is a nominal $3.00 to fish. Rental tackle, bait and other fishing supplies are available. Completion of a new 1300 foot pier is projected for 1997.

There are basically three different kinds of fishing available on the pier. Moving from the beach Gulfward, these include: 1) bottom fishing in the troughs between the sandbars just off the beach; 2) bottom and top water fishing on the outer bar that runs perpendicular to the pier several hundred feet out; and 3) and to a limited extent, top water fishing off the end of the pier.

A variety of good eating and great fighting fish can be caught in the close-in troughs. In the Spring and again in the Fall, both Flounder and Pompano show up in increasing numbers. They join the Whiting which routinely inhabit this water.

Midway out on the pier, fishing the bar that parallels the beach provides a different set of challenges. A variety of species can be found on and adjacent to the bar including Spanish and Northern Mackerel, Bluefish, Flounder, Cobia and from time to time, Jack Cravalle. The first four of these are good eating, while all put up superior fights.

The deep water end of the pier can offer superb big game fishing. King Mackerel up to 50 pounds, Cobia almost as big, Blackfin Tuna up to 30 pounds plus, and Tarpon over 100 pounds are not at all unusual. Dolphin and Sailfish have also been landed on the end of the pier, before it was shortened by the hurricanes.

Inshore

Of all the kinds of fishing available in the Destin area, Inshore trolling and bottom fishing are clearly the most popular. This can probably attributed to two basic factors. The first is the proximity of quality fish. For example, very large King Mackerel and Cobia, lots of Spanish Mackerel, etc., etc., can all be caught within five miles of the beach. The second factor is the large number of relatively small boats in the area that can usually be taken safely into the Gulf. Put the two factors together, and it's easy to understand the popularity of Inshore fishing.

As was true for the Pensacola area, we've arbitrarily defined inshore Destin waters as the area from the outer bar along the beach to about five miles out. Water depths range from 25 feet close to shore to as much as 100 feet in a few spots farther out. For the most part, the bottom is devoid of significant natural bottom structure.

Accordingly, what little natural structure there is and any artificial structure subsequently installed by man quickly draws a very fishy crowd. This structure and other points of interest are highlighted on the following maps. Although the maps are not to scale, they do highlight the proximity of many good spots for small boat fishermen.

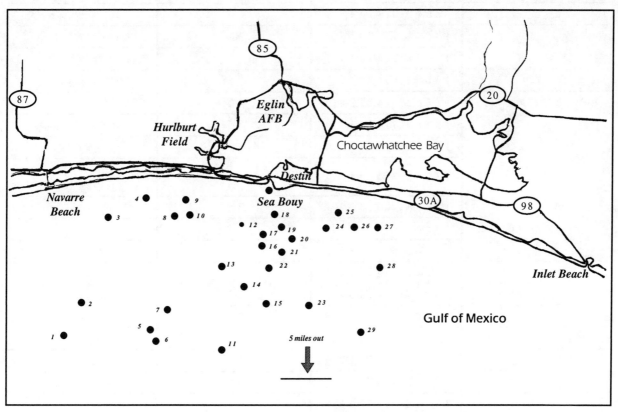

Figure 2.14 - **Destin Area Inshore Waters**

The majority of time, the entire area covered by the map can be easily and safely fished in a relatively small boat. In stormy or excessively windy weather, however, just getting out through the mouth of East Pass can be harrowing, if not plain dangerous. Before heading out the Pass, and as a minimum, always check for small craft advisories and whether or not the charter boat fleet has gone out. If it hasn't, you know the Gulf is no place for a small boat that day.

Spot #	LORAN Coordinates	Depth (ft)	Name/ Structure
1	13587.1/47116.6	66	Tire modules
2	13611.2/47120.1	65	Unknown
3	13623.6/47134.2	63	Unknown
4	13640.0/47137.0	60	Unknown
5/6	13648.1/47115.9	87	Liberty Ship
	13648.2/47115.7		Thomas Hayward
7	13656.8/47119.7	73	Unknown
8/9/10	13660.1/47134.9	70	Boxcars
	13664.7/47137.9	50	Pole Spot
	13665.0/47135.0	50	Boxcars
	13660.7/47134.1	80	200' Brown Barge
	13664.7/47137.7	75	Pier Rubble
	13664.9/47138.0	75	Pier Rubble
	13665.6/47138.2	75	Pier Rubble
11	13680.2/47114.2	80	Unknown
12	13697.0/47134.6	60	The Billy
13	13690.5/47127.8	70	Unknown
14	13700.2/47123.2	72	Cars
15	13708.1/47119.9	75	Rubble
16	13715.1/47130.9	66	Boxcars
17	13715.3/47132.8	64	Boxcars
18	13717.9/47136.7	50	Bridge Rubble
19/20	13720.9/47132.8	72	100' Barge
	13720.8/47132.6	65	100' Barge
21/22	13720.4/47131.0	73	Bridge Rubble
	13720.3/47130.6	60	Bridge Rubble
23	13722.0/47119.7	74	Unknown
24	13753.0/47131.9	65	Cars, scrap metal, tires
25	13766.0/47135.0		Concrete, appliances, tires
26	13765.7/47132.2	60	Boxcars
	13766.0/47134.5	65	Fuel tanks
27	13773.1/47132.1	60	Box cars
28	13771.1/47122.8	72	Unknown
29	13754.0/47111.0	78	Unknown

Figure 2.15 - **Inshore Spot Location Coordinates**

The data on the Inshore Fishing Spots is designed for use for LORAN equipped boats. The LORAN coordinates are uncorrected for plotting on navigational charts. Also, and due to the varying approach of local artificial reef programs on reporting location by LORAN coordinates, there can be no guarantee that the numbers provided correspond to the center of deployed material. If, when trying to locate an artificial reef, your depth finder does not indicate material on the bottom, start a circular search pattern and gradually expand it until material is located.

Although not shown in the table, one additional set of LORAN coordinates are worthy of mention: 13656.7/ 47135.7 This is the location of a 140 foot by 30 foot steel barge loaded with scrap iron and storage tanks that was recently sunk off the Okaloosa Island Pier (two miles South Southwest).

Each of the spots shown on the map and described in the table is potentially productive for both bottom fishing and as an area for trolling. Because these spots are close in, they do get worked hard by bottom fishermen looking for Amberjack, Cobia, Snapper, and occasional Grouper and Triggerfish. Nevertheless, each is worth a try for a nice fat, fresh fish for the evening's dinner table.

In the Spring, sight fishing for Cobia during their Westward migration provides lots of local excitement. At this time of year, these fish do not relate to structure. Instead, their movement is close-in, usually from just outside the outer bar to about a half mile off the beach. In the late Fall, however, a different pattern prevails. During this period, the fish are headed Eastward, usually several miles offshore. During this movement, they have a tendency to stop and visit at bottom structure along their route of travel. Bottom fishermen working the spots on the map sometimes do well on these Cobia.

Like Fall Cobia, one frequently used trolling route for King Mackerel can also be related to bottom structure. The route has proven particularly effective when the fish are playing hard to get in one or more specific spots. It begins at the Sea Buoy, moves SE to #18 (Bridge Rubble), then on out to the #19, 20, 21, 16, and 17 area. If you haven't limited by then, head roughly WNW to #12 (The Billy). From there, continue West to #10 and #8 and then into #9 (Pole Spot). If you still haven't limited, head North to the area around the Okaloosa Island Pier. By now, you'll surely have all the Kings you want, perhaps a Blackfin Tuna or two, and more than likely, some Bonito. So, head East back toward the Pass about 200 yards off the beach. You can probably pick up some nice Spanish Mackerel on your way back to port!

If you're not into long distance trolling, spend your time in the immediate area of the Sea Buoy. This area routinely produces a good variety of fish for trollers and those drifting with live bait. At different times during the year, this has included King, Spanish and Northern Mackerel, Cobia, Amberjack, Bonito and Sailfish.

In addition to the spots identified above, several others have been added to Destin waters in recent years. They're highlighted in figure 2.16.

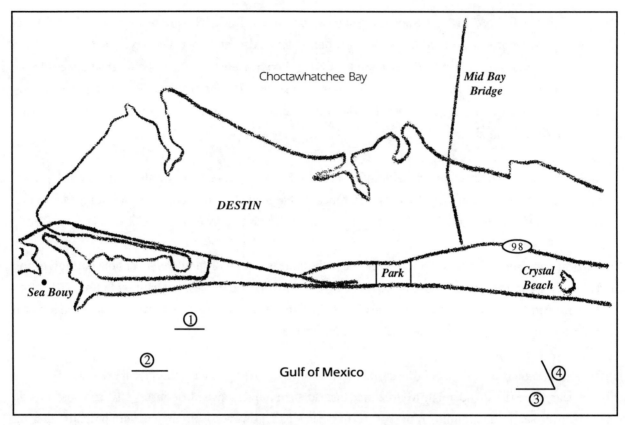

Figure 2.16 - **New Destin Area Inshore Reefs**

①   One mile off the East end of Destin Harbor. Named the 10 Fathom Reef. Consists of 80 five foot tall concrete pyramids sunk in a line 750 feet long. The western end of the reef is one mile from the mouth of East Pass on a heading of 125 degrees. LORAN coordinates for the reef are: West end- 13721.5/47139.1; East end- 13723.0/47139.1

②   Fish Haven #2 (A Leg). This leg is 4500 feet long and about 1 ½ miles off Destin harbor. It consists of rubble from Mid-Bay Bridge and concrete pyramids and is slightly more than one mile South-Southeast of the tip of the East jetty. This leg is in 60-68 feet of water. LORAN coordinates: West end- 13713.0/47136.0; East end: 13723.0/47136.0

③④   (B and C legs.) They're located one nautical mile Southeast of Crystal Beach. Same composition and depth as the A leg. The B leg is 3,600 feet long and the C leg is 3,300 feet long. The concrete pyramids were placed on the bottom in clusters of four, 180 feet apart. LORAN coordinates: B leg- 13765.0/47132.8 and 13772.0/47132.8; C leg- 13772.0/47135.5 and 13772.0/47132.8

In addition to these superb fish attraction sites, nine M-60 Army battle tanks have also been emplaced in Destin area Inshore waters in the last couple of years.

• Two miles South-Southeast of the Okaloosa Island Pier/LORAN: 13662.7/47135.3; 13663.6/47135.6; 13663.9/47135.5; 13664.0/47135.5

- One and one half miles Southeast of the Okaloosa Island Pier/LORAN: 13667.6/47137.6; and, 13667.7/47137.7

- One and one half miles Southeast of East Pass jetties/LORAN: 13720.2/47134.2

- Two miles South of Crystal Beach: 13762.2/47132.9; and, 13763.0/47132.9

As a final but fundamentally obvious note, while fishing Inshore, keep your eyes on the charter boats. The professionals that run these boats have the experience and sophisticated electronics to always find the fish. Watch them, emulate what they do, and stay with them. But, most importantly, don't get in their way while they're making their living. In this regard, when you see a group of charter boats working a particular area, DO NOT head for the middle of them. Lay back and look for the pattern of movement. More often than not, they will be following each other in some sort of circle. If this is the case, start your own circle just outside theirs. You'll catch plenty of fish-- while not provoking an incident at sea.

Offshore

Offshore fishing in the Destin area seems to have one thing in common with fishing in the Choctawhatchee Bay. It's underdeveloped. Although there is an abundance of big game and bottom fish available at various times from five miles on out, the tendency of most fishermen seems to be to stay Inshore. Historically, there have just been too many great opportunities close-in to spend the extra time and money going Offshore to chase the big guys.

As noted earlier, Destin shares the superb big game trolling area around Desoto Canyon with both Pensacola and Panama City. Accordingly, it was described earlier in the Pensacola section and is omitted here. The remainder of this section, however, will be devoted to the superior year round bottom fishing available in Destin area waters. Figure 2.17 identifies a number of proven bottom spots. Although its not to scale, the map does provide a useful perspective on the geographical dispersion of deep water sites.

In addition to the spots highlighted on the Offshore map and characterized in Figure 2.18, there are some other sites that may be of interest. They include:

- Five U.S. Army M-60 tanks located 13 miles South-Southeast of the East Pass jetties: 13742.0/47053.1; 13742.6/47052.8; 13750.2/47050.1; 13756.6/47047.8; and, 13765.1/47048.0

- White Hill Reef, six nautical miles West-Southwest of East Pass in 75-80 feet of water: 13660.9/47119.5

- Frangista Reef, eleven nautical miles East of the Pass in 80 feet of water: 13785.5/47118.2

- Timberholes, twenty to twenty-five nautical miles Southwest of the Pass in 105-110 feet of water: 13480.8/47074.6

- Big AJ Reef, six nautical miles South-Southeast of the Pass in 80 feet of water: 13722.1/47122.0

- Butt Head Tug, 85 feet of water: 13570.2/47102.6

- Sailboat Wreck, 80 feet of water: 13588.4/47106.2

- Mingo Ridge, 215 feet of water: 13624.9/46998.2

- No Name, 20 nm South-Southeast of Destin Pass, 140 feet of water, two tons of concrete pipe, six locations with 10-15 pieces of pipe each: 13739.8/47030.0; 13749.7/47025.1; 13759.6/47019.9; 13770.0/47015.0; 13780.1/47010.1; and, 13769.3/47010.1

- New Valparaiso Reef. This new bottom spot was constructed out of 385 tons of mostly intact four foot concrete culvert sections;. The new spot is located about 13.5 nautical miles South-Southeast of the East Pass sea bouy in 109 feet of water. LORAN: 13739.8/47059.0

And that will hopefully give you a good start on productive Offshore bottom fishing spots in the Destin area. We'll take a look at the Panama City area in the next section.

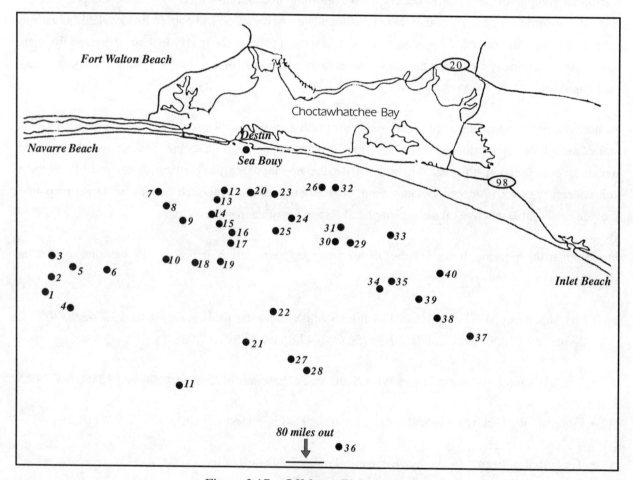

Figure 2.17 - **Offshore Fishing Spots**

Spot#	LORAN coordinates	Depth (ft)	Name/Structure
1	13270.10/47024.5	144	Tires, appliance
2	13300.4/47010.1	138	Trucks, cabs
3	13330.0/47020.0	150	Unknown
4	13170.0/46897.0	800	"Elbow"
5	Lat30/02/02C Long87/00/01C		Hilpert's Site 4
6	13305.0/46965.0	600	"Nipple"
7	13500.0/47090.0		Unknown
8	13515.2/47083.9	85	440' Liberty Ship "Joseph E. Brown"
9	13544.0/47062.3	118	Barge "Teen's Reef"
10	13536.0/47042.0	130	Tire modules
11	13342.0/46805.0	2400	"Spur"
12	13600.2/47094.0	78	Unknown
13	13535.9/47064.2		Liquid storage tanks (1)
	13534.7/47060.7		Liquid storage tanks (3)
	13534.4/47061.5		Liquid storage tanks (5)
	13533.4/47064.8		Liquid storage tanks (7)
	13533.4/47062.8		Liquid storage tanks (1)
	13532.8/47071.6		Liquid storage tanks (4)
	13532.6/47062.5		Liquid storage tanks (7)
	13531.7/47063.7		Liquid storage tanks (3)
	13531.4/47064.5		Liquid storage tanks (3)
	13531.1/47064.1		Liquid storage tanks (2)
	13530.5/47062.0		Liquid storage tanks (4)
	13530.2/47062.4		Liquid storage tanks (4)
14	13464.7/47040.9	160	Rock Cliffs
15	13592.0/47066.0	98	Unknown
16	13600.0/47062.0	100	Tire modules
17	13550.0/46975.0	375	"Flats"
18	13565.2/47024.5	200	Boat hulls, tires, PVC pipe
19	13597.0/47028.0	172	Unknown
20	1365.0/47090.0		Unknown
21	13602.3/46967.2	180	Target Ship
22	Lat 29/59/36C Long 86/30/20C		Unknown
23	13720.0/Long 86/29/54C		Unknown
24	13738.4/47041.5	115	Coral Reef
25	13700.0/45050.0	100	Tire modules
26	13771.9/47089.4	90	19' boat filled with scrap metal
27	Lat29/53/09C Long 86/24/02C		Unknown
28	13783.4/47123.3		3 steel cages filled with tires
29	13800.0/47050.0	100	Tire modules
30	13786.4/47054.6	102	Landing Craft
31	13785.0/47058.0		Boat hulls, appliances, junk
32	13800.0/47090.0		Unknown
33	13877.0/47050.0	110	10 fiberglass boat hulls
34	13853.5/47022.0		Unknown
35	13858.5/47014.0	106	Unknown
36	13700.0/46800.0	384	Tire Bundles
37	13950.0/46910.0	110	Tire Modules
38	13902.5/46959.2	99	Unknown
39	13891.1/46991.7	105	Steel tug, tire bundles
	13890.0/46990.0	105	Fiberglass boat parts
40	13900.0/47017.0	97	Unknown

Figure 2.18 - **Offshore Spot Location Coordinates**

PANAMA CITY AREA

Continuing to the East, this third segment of the Florida *Panhandle* includes the area from Inlet Beach to the Eastern boundary of Tyndall Air Force Base. In between these two locations, there is a real diversity of topography, bottom structure, and variety in the kinds of potentially productive waters to fish. There are some 20 miles of Gulf beaches similar to those farther West in the Panhandle. There are also four significant bays included in the Panama City area, along with feeder creeks, a sound, several islands, and old and new passes into the Gulf of Mexico. All this, and Desoto Canyon Offshore big game waters are only a couple of hours running time to the Southwest. Given this diversity, and not surprisingly, fishing in Panama City area waters is extraordinary year round. Figure 2.19 provides a bird's eye view of the area.

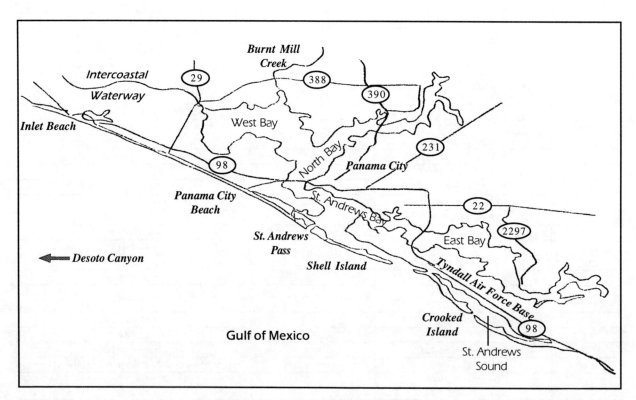

Figure 2.19 - **The Panama City Area**

Figure 2.20 reflects the same kind of catch data presented in Chapter 1. In this case, however, the focus is only on reported activity in the Panama City area. The data in the summary was derived from the fishing reports published in *Panhandle* newspapers and other publications over the last several years.

The monthly fishing activity highlighted in Figure 2.20 has necessarily been generalized. Based on historical experience, it suggests reasonable expectations for any given kind of fish in any given month. The following narrative sharpens up this focus. It describes Panama City area fishing activity on a month-by-month basis using relatively current specific catch data obtained from area tackle stores, bait shops, landings, etc. Many of the locations identified in the data will be highlighted in the sections that follow.

Panhandle Gamefish	J	F	M	A	M	J	J	A	S	O	N	D
Amberjack	X			XX		XX	XX	X	X	X	X	
Black Drum	XX	X				X			X	XX	XX	XX
Black Sea Bass	XX	XX	X		XX	X	X			X	X	XX
Blackfin Tuna				X		X		XX				
Bluefish	XX	XX	XX	X	X	X	XXX	XX	XX	XX	X	X
Blue Marlin							X	XX	XX	X		
Bonito				XX	XXX	XX	XXX	XX	XX			
Cobia			XX	XXX	XXX	XX	XX	XX	X			
Dolphin						X	XX	XX	XXX	XX		
Flounder	X	X	XX	X	X	X	XX	XX	XXX	XX	X	
Grouper	XX	X	X	XX	X	X	XX	X	XX	XX	XX	XX
Jack Cravalle											XX	
King Mackerel			X	X	XX	XXX	XXX	XX	XX	XX	X	
Northern Mackerel			X	X	X	X						
Pompano				XX	XXX	XX	X	X	X			
Redfish	X	X	X	XX	XX	XXX	XX	XX	XXX	XX	XX	X
Sailfish					X	X	X	XX	XX			
Sheepshead	XXX	XX				X			X	XX	XX	XXX
Snapper	XX	XX	XX	X	XX	XX	XX	X	XX	XXX		
Spanish Mackerel			XX	XXX	XX	XXX	XXX	XX	XX	XX	XX	
Swordfish												
Tarpon						X	XX	X	XX	X		
Triggerfish								X	X	X		
Tripletail					XX	X	X					
Trout	X	X	XX	XXX	XXX	XX	XX	XX	XXX	XX	X	X
Wahoo			X		XX	X	XX	XX	XX	X		
White Marlin						X	XX	X	X			
Whiting						XX			X	XX	XX	
Yellowfin Tuna							X	X	XX	X		

Legend: Blank= No reported activity XX= Good catches reported during the month

X= At least a few reported caught in the area during the month XXX= Great. Even if you just do a few things right, you're going to catch fish

Figure 2.20 - **Panama City Area Annual Fishing Summary**

January

- Sheepshead and Black Drum on pilings and bridge supports in the Panama City local area.
- Bluefish and Sea Bass in St. Andrews Bay.
- Grouper and Snapper in 60-100 feet of water (within five miles of the Panama City sea buoys).

- Sheepshead below the Dear Point Lake Dam.
- Trout and Reds in area rivers, at the heads of bayous and in tidal creeks.
- AJ's on the "Zina" wreck in 180 feet of water off Mexico Beach.
- Groupers on Pigfish in St. Andrews Bay.
- Off Panama City, Flounder on Inshore Gulf wrecks.
- ACMI TIS towers off Mexico Beach good for Grouper, Amberjack and Flounder.
- Sea Bass off the St. Andrews Pass jetties.
- Sheepshead on shallow Inshore wrecks in 25-50 feet of water.

February

- Good trolling for Grouper in 15-30 feet of water over structures.
- Dan Russell Pier: Black Drum and Sheepshead.
- Flounder on sand bottoms off the Gulf beach of Shell Island.
- Specs and Reds in Burnt Mill Creek on West Bay north of Panama City.
- Flounder on artificial structure East of St. Andrews Pass.
- Sheepshead everywhere on bridges and pilings.
- Sea Bass off the jetties in St. Andrews Pass.

March

- Dan Russell Pier: Spanish, Cobia, Pompano, Bonito.
- Bluefish and Spanish at the St. Andrews Pass jetties and on the "Camelbacks" in the bay.
- Red Snapper on shallow water wrecks in less than 100 feet of water.
- Big Specs starting to show inside Crooked Island.
- Reds and Specs at the mouth of Burnt Mill Creek.
- Flounder around boat docks and pilings.
- Cobia off to a good start along the beaches.

April

- Pompano just starting to show in the Surf in the Panama City area.
- Cobia around structure in the East and along the beach to the West.
- Kings starting to show Inshore.
- Some big Kings, Wahoo and Blackfin Tuna on deepwater bottom spots on live bait.
- Specs on grassflats, bayous and river mouths.
- Spanish, Pompano, Cobia and Bonito starting to show well off the Dan Russell Pier.
- Grouper, Snapper and Amberjack on shallow water structure off Mexico Beach.
- Spanish around the St. Andrews Pass jetties and along the beach.

May

- A few big Kings along the beaches.
- Cobia plentiful outside the outer bar moving West.
- Pompano thick in the area surf.
- Spanish beginning to show Inshore.
- Big Reds around the pilings of the Tyndall bridge.

- Sailfish in 30-50 fathoms of water.
- Dan Russell Pier: Spanish, Cobia, Pompano, Bonito and Bluefish.

June

- Kings on Inshore reefs early.
- Snapper, Grouper and AJ's on structure in 40-100 feet of water.
- Specs on all grassflats.
- Dolphin, Wahoo, White Marlin, Sailfish and Blackfin Tuna in 30-60 fathoms of water.
- Russell pier yielding Kings, Pompano, Flounder, Bonito, Spanish and Bluefish.
- Pompano, Reds, Whiting, Sheepshead and Black Drum in the Surf early and late in the day.
- Triggers, "Mingos" and AJ's on structure in 60-90 feet of water.
- Dan Russell Pier: Spanish, Kings, Blues and Bonito.
- Cobia in St. Andrews Bay between the Passes and on structure.
- Spanish along the beach, in the Pass, and scattered in area bays.

July

- Kings around the mouth of St. Andrews Pass.
- Grouper, Snapper and AJ's along the "edge of the 29 fathom curve and at the "21 Rocks".
- Bonito everywhere Inshore.
- Dan Russell Pier: Spanish, Blues and Kings.
- Specs on the grass flats in West Bay early and late.
- Schoolie Dolphin along Inshore weed lines.
- Spanish on the Camelbacks in St. Andrews Bay.

August

- Marlin, Wahoo and Tuna in the Loop Current.
- Big Sharks in the Surf at night on very large chunks of Bonito.
- Dan Russell Pier: Spanish and Blues.
- Specs around lighted docks at night.
- Cobia moving East along the buoy line wrecks off Mexico Beach.
- Amberjack on the "Empire Mica".
- Wahoo, White Marlin, Sailfish and Blackfin Tuna Offshore on the "Swanson", "Madison" and "Johnny Walker" coral domes.
- Spanish and Kings on the car body reefs.
- Trolling productive for schooling Spanish and Bluefish in St. Andrews Bay.
- Grouper, Snapper, and Amberjack on shallow water Inshore wrecks.
- Blackfin Tuna around the mouth of St. Andrews Pass.

September

- Kings on the JC and car body reefs and along the buoy line off Mexico Beach.
- Flounder on and around structure in all bays.
- Blue and White Marlin, Wahoo, and Yellowfin Tuna deep on live bait in Desoto Canyon.
- In the Surf, Sheepshead, Black Drum, Whiting and Reds in the deeper troughs along the beach.

- Many White Marlin and some Blue Marlin in the Desoto Canyon area.
- Dolphin and Wahoo within 10 miles of the shore along weed lines.
- King Mackerel on Inshore structure.
- Dan Russell Pier: Spanish, Kings, Flounder, Blues and Sailfish.
- Red Snapper and Gag Grouper moving into area water less than 100 feet deep.
- Cobia, Grouper in St. Andrew's Bay. Spanish on the "Camelbacks".

October

- Blue and White Marlin feeding aggressively Offshore.
- Dolphin and Wahoo on Inshore weedlines.
- Spanish Mackerel schooling close-in. Watch for birds/bait.
- Grouper and Snapper on structure in 90-120 feet of water.
- Trout back on the grass flats in St. Andrews Bay around high tide.
- In the East, Kings in 40-50 feet of water.
- Schoolie Dolphin along the buoy line off Mexico Beach.
- Dan Russell Pier: Kings, Blues, Flounder, Sheepshead and Spanish.
- Grouper on wrecks and rock piles in St. Andrews Bay.
- Specs and Reds heading up area rivers and creeks.

November

- Sheepshead and Bluefish all over the St. Andrews jetties.
- Grouper and Amberjack on wrecks in 75 feet of water.
- Red Snapper on Inshore wrecks off St. Andrews Pass.
- Specs and Reds moving upstream in creeks and rivers.
- Grouper in 30-60 feet of water off Mexico Beach.
- Kingfish off Mexico Beach along the buoy line and over the "Car Bodies" area. Also at the mouth of St. Andrews Pass.
- Dan Russell Pier: Whiting, Blues.
- Cobia on Inshore Panama City wrecks.
- Specs in Burnt Mill Creek.

December

- Black Sea Bass on Inshore wrecks/reefs in less than 70 feet of water.
- Flounder spawning on Inshore reefs.
- Sheepshead all over most pilings in most bays.
- Grouper and Snapper in 100 feet of water and on out.
- Whiting and Blues off the Dan Russell Pier.
- Blues on the "Camelbacks" in St. Andrews Bay.
- Sheepshead off the jetties in St. Andrews Pass.

With that overview of what species bites when in mind, it's now time to get specific about where to fish. We'll focus on the five generic types of fishing available in the Panama City area: Bay, Surf, Piers, Inshore and Offshore. In the process of looking at each of these, maps, charts and navigation data will be presented to help you find the good spots to try. Panama City bays and adjacent waters will be described first.

Bays

Figure 2.21 just begins to identify all the points that might interest you in and around Panama City. The diversity of available year round fishing in area bays and adjacent waters is extraordinary. Hopefully, the points identified in the figure will at least get you started in the right direction.

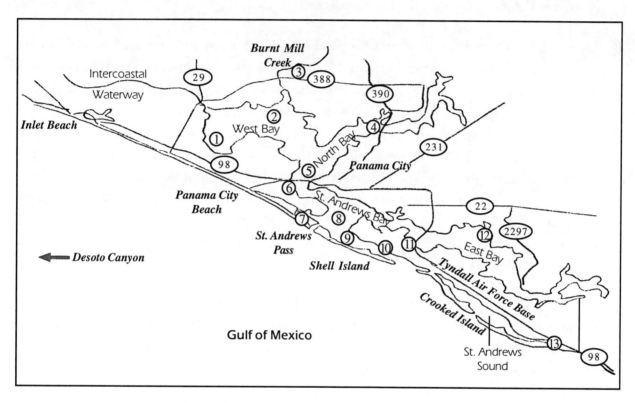

Figure 2.21 - **Panama City Area Bays**

Legend

①   West Bay. Good grass flats along the South side. Downstream from the drawbridge over the Hot Water Canal is a good area for Specs.

②   Mouths of Hot Water Canal, Burnt Mill Creek, and Crooked Creek excellent Spring Spec fishing. At various other times of the year, Reds and Flounder will hang out there too.

③   Burnt Mill Creek. There's a boat ramp close to Highway 388 bridge over the creek. Great late Fall/ Winter Spec/Red fishing. Fish the deepest holes you can find--very slowly.

④   Deerpoint Dam. The area below the dam is routinely good for monster seven to nine pound Sheepshead and Black Drum in the Spring.

⑤   Northeast side of Hathaway Bridge. Good grass flats. Start your drift one quarter mile North and drift down to the bridge. Also, there's a nice roadside park on both sides of the West end of the bridge. Great access to the deep water of the nearby channel.

⑥   Naval Coastal Systems Center. You must have a Department of Defense (DOD) sticker on your car. Access off either Thomas Road or Hwy 98. Great facilities including a boat ramp on St. Andrews Bay. Boat rentals. Shore fisherman can use the helicopter and ammo docks. The big guys including Kings, Cobia, and Grouper are a distinct possibility.

⑦   St. Andrews State Park. A fisherman's paradise. This 1260 acre park offers a variety of fishing opportunities to the visiting angler. On its North side, there is a fishing pier into Grand Lagoon which consistently yields Specs, Reds, and Flounder amongst other things. The crabbing is also excellent. The East end of the park is bounded by St. Andrews Pass and its year round superb fishing opportunities. Convenient parking for jetty fishermen is available at the Jetty store. Surf fishermen are not forgotten. The Park has over a mile of Gulf front beach available. Pompano, Spanish, Bluefish, and Whiting are always possibilities. A final feature offered by the Park is unique. Both in-season and off, a shuttle boat is available to carry visitors to Shell Island. You can stay as long as you want on the island, and round trip tickets are only $7.50 for adults and $5.50 for kids. Among other things, there is great surf and bay fishing available. There is a $4.00/car park entrance fee, and bait and tackle are available at park stores.

⑧   Cobia and Grouper fishing in St. Andrews Bay. For Cobia, fish around structure in deep water (40 feet) South of Highway 98 (Hathaway) Bridge and between the two Passes into the bay. For Grouper, fish wrecks and rock piles in the Bay. A couple of spots you might want to try: 1) five steel hulled lifeboats in 25 feet of water - LORAN 14101.7/46987.4; and, 2) 150 foot "Spanish Shanty" tar barge in 18 feet of water - 14101.4/46895.1.

⑨   Camelback. Large area of sand humps in St. Andrews Bay. Grass flats surrounded by deep water. Run down the middle of the old Pass. Off to the sides, the white spots you see are sand areas between grass beds. Beds are four to eight feet deep. Trolling the Camelback area usually productive for a variety of fish.

⑩   Tyndall Marina. This Air Force Base is divided in half by Hwy 98. A DOD vehicle sticker is required for access to either the North or South sides of the base. The Tyndall Marina is on the South Side. It's located on that stretch of St. Andrews Bay that connects the old and new St. Andrews Passes. Superior shore fishing from the Marina jetties can produce even the biggest local inhabitants including King Mackerel, Cobia, Spanish, Blues, and oversized Redfish. Excellent boat ramps.

⑪   Two areas of interest here. First, there are North and South sections of the old Tyndall bridge available for fishing. Both sections provide fishermen access to the deep water channel of the Intercoastal

Waterway, which runs down the middle of East Bay. Second, Tyndall's Bonita Bay Recreation Area is located at the Southern end of the new East Bay Bridge. Although access to the area is not controlled, cars using it are expected to have DOD stickers. Bonita Bay has a variety of boats to rent, good shore fishing spots, and excellent boat ramps.

⑫   East Bay and other Panama City wade fishing locations. A boat helps in getting to many of the prime wading spots. Fish drop-offs along points and sand bars. Specific spots of interest in East Bay and adjacent St. Andrews Bay waters include:

By Boat:
- Piney Point, East Bay. The East side of the point is most productive. Fish from the point of land and for about 300-yards North--not from the large sandbar.
- Smith Point to Laird Point, East Bay--The entire bank should produce fish. Cedar Point, East Bay--The East and West sides; nice sharp drop off can be found here.
- Palmetto Point, Tyndall AFB-- Both the East and West sides produce fish.
- Davis Point, St. Andrews Bay, Tyndall AFB--North and South sides offer good spots.
- Breakfast Point to Long Point, North Bay--One mile long, shallow, narrow bar, drops off to five feet and is good when fishing artificials.
- Shell Island--Concentrate on the North side of the island.

By Car:
- St. Andrews State Park Recreation Area, Panama City Beach--At the old army dock, the flat on the West side of the dock behind the campground is a good spot. Try in the mornings and late afternoons.
- Coral Gray Park, Hathaway Bridge--On the East side of the bridge, fish the long flat.
- Buena Vista Point to Lake Caroline, St. Andrews Bay--Fish the flat. Access off Alternate Highway 98.
- Mouth of Lake Hampton, St. Andrews Bay--Access off Michigan Avenue. If you're going to use a boat to get to wading spots, boat ramps are available at the DuPont (Tyndall) Bridge, Callaway Bayou at the Callaway Men's Club, Cook Bayou at Fred Williams Landing, and at St. Andrews State Park.

⑬   Crooked Island/St. Andrew Sound. Located off Highway 98 on the East side of Tyndall AFB. Turn South at the Air Force sign that says"Wright Laboratory Air Base Technology." The turn off is about three miles before you get to Mexico Beach. Boat ramp. Good flats. White sand bottom and very clean water makes sight fishing possible. In addition to usual catch (Specs, Reds, Flounder, Pompano), Sharks always a possibility due to immediate access from the Gulf.

So much for the bays, bayous, sounds, and lagoons in and around Panama City. Given the expanse of potentially productive water, other possibilities are limitless. But, we must move on. Let's go Surf fishing!

Surf

Surf fishing in the Panama City area can be superb during much of the year. Potentially productive surf stretches some 38 miles from Inlet Beach in the West to the Eastern tip of Shell Island. Despite extensive development along a portion of this stretch, there is still considerable undeveloped gulf front land, adequate road-side parking, and public beach access walkovers in even the most developed areas.

The topography of Panama City area surf is much the same as that found farther West in the Destin and Pensacola areas. The beach slopes down to a trough which more or less parallels the shore. The first of two sandbars is on the far side of the trough, and, it too, parallels the beach. A second trough is on the far side of the first sandbar and a second sandbar is on the far side of that one. The flat sandy bottom of the Gulf begins beyond the second bar. For the most part, this pattern still persists despite the ravages of recent hurricanes.

Cuts in bars, perpendicular to the beach, are also present and can be identified in two ways. The first is to look for darker colored water extending out into the Gulf across the bars. The second, if there are waves breaking, is to look for spots where they don't break, indicating an absence of the bar. Cuts occur randomly along the beach and provide a way for fish to come in to the troughs along the beach to feed. All of these features are relatively easy to see from the beach due to the differences in water color.

From a surf fishing standpoint, bottom contour is fundamentally important because it tells you where to fish. The name of the game in the Panama City area is to fish the cuts and troughs. Although there may be times during higher tides when fish chase bait across bars, the majority of the time they'll use the cuts to come in to feed in the relatively deeper waters of the troughs.

In addition to the surf fish identified in the Species/Location Correlation Matrix presented in Chapter 1, non-edible species also frequent the Panama City area surf and provide excellent sport. Those include a variety of Jacks, Ladyfish, Saltwater Catfish, Sharks and Stingrays. And there's always a chance for a surprise-- like the isolated Cobia or King Mackerel that is caught now and then in the surf!

When to fish is an easy question to address for the Panama City area surf because the answer is clear cut. Although something may bite throughout the day (and night), all fish seem to bite best at three specific times. The first is at sunup, regardless of what the tide is doing. The second is around sundown, also regardless of the tide. The third is during the two hour period that precedes the high tide. If you have to choose only one of these three periods to fish, sunup is absolutely the best.

A few words about wind and its effects on the surf may also be helpful. Generally, Southeast, South and Southwest winds of up to 10-15mph are good. They make waves in the Gulf. As these waves break over the bars, they churn up the sand and release the food that it holds-- like sandfleas, crabs, etc. Hungry fish aren't far behind. Winds from any Northerly heading, however, do just the opposite. They generally stifle any wave action along the beach. As a result, food is not exposed and any fish in the area are not motivated to feed. The effects of winds from the East and West are really problematical. Sometimes fishing results are good-- and sometimes they're not. If in doubt, you can't tell without throwing in a line. Some places to try are highlighted in Figure 2.22.

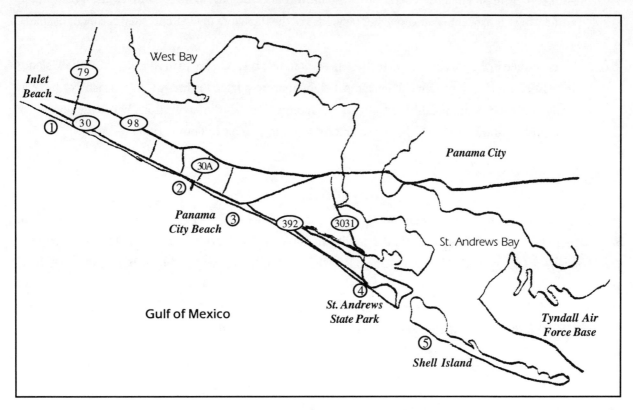

Figure 2.22 - **Panama City Area Surf**

Legend

①   There is an excellent stretch of surf in an area called Laguna Beach. As of the Summer of '96, the bar and trough structure is very uniform and there are a number of easily visible cuts in the bars. Best of all, there is an obvious hole about 30 yards off the beach that consistently holds big Pompano, Flounder, and Redfish. The hole is about where County road 3087 hits Highway 30.

②   Farther into town, the surf on either side of the Dan Russell pier is always worth a try. The pier is a natural magnet for all gamefish in the area. Frequently, a surf fisherman can intercept approaching schools before they are within range of the pier. Pier parking is across the street and bait/tackle are available at the foot of the pier.

③   This is the location of the remnants of the former county pier. Much of the old structure still exists and continues to serve as a powerful fish attractor. There is ample off road parking adjacent to the former pier. There is a nice bar/trough structure along this stretch of beach.

④   This mile long stretch of beach within the St. Andrews State Park can be immensely productive. Given its proximity to St. Andrews Pass, its not surprising to see many species of fish not normally known to inhabit the surf. The "fishiness" of this water is further enhanced by yet another former pier. Although there isn't much left of the old St. Andrews Park Gulf pier, there is enough to draw bait, which attracts bigger fish, etc. You know the story. Park at the Pier store in the Southwest corner of the park.

⑤   As described in the previous Bays section, there is shuttle boat service to the uninhabited Shell Island. In season, a surf fisherman can have almost eight hours to pursue the many kinds of fish available in the island's surf or around the East jetty of St. Andrews Pass. Just a suggestion--watch the tide tables carefully. You want to be on the island and fishing during the two hour period preceding high tide.

Dan Russell Pier

Panama City has one of the two remaining Gulf piers in the entire Florida ***Panhandle***. It is called the Dan Russell pier and it is world renowned for the quality and diversity of the fishing it offers. The pier is located just about where county road 30H (off Coleman Rd.) deadends into Highway 30 on the beach. It is over 1600 feet in length, all concrete, fully lighted, and some 62 species of fish have been caught off it. The admission charge is $3.00 for adults and $2.00 for kids. Bait and rental tackle are available. The pier is open 24 hours a day except for Wednesdays and Thursdays, when it closes at midnight and reopens at 6:00am the next morning.

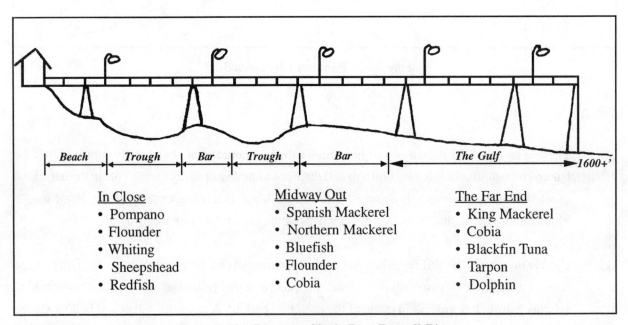

Figure 2.23 - **Panama City's Dan Russell Pier**

Figure 2.23 provides some insights that may be useful to you. First, the various kinds of fish contained in the three groupings do not necessarily recognize the artificial boundaries suggested in the drawing. Accordingly, you don't ever want to leave a line in the water and your rod and reel unattended. You never know when a

40 pound Cobia is going to swim along the inner through eating sand fleas--and not realize you were fishing for Pompano! Second, be prepared. As noted in Chapter 3, it's frequently a good idea to have two different kinds of tackle with you on the pier. Then, for example, if you are fishing relatively light mid-way out for Spanish---and the Kings attack---you can successfully enjoy that fun too.

Finally, as the figure indicates, the pier is more than a quarter mile long. That's a long way if you've got to lug all your stuff on your back. Smart guys use a variety of wheeled vehicles including everything from little red wagons to shopping carts to pretty sophisticated, custom built conveyances.

So much for the Dan Russell pier. It can and routinely does provide great fishing opportunities. It also offers delightful surprises now and then--like monster Sharks and the spectacular Sailfish. And, you can't beat the price. We'll now take a look at Inshore fishing in the Panama City Area.

Inshore

There is real diversity in Inshore fishing opportunities across the Panama City area. This is fundamentally the result of the amount of artificial and natural structure present in any particular stretch of Inshore water. Figure 2.24 makes the point. From Inlet beach to past Mexico Beach, extensive artificial reef building has resulted in many good spots for both trolling and bottom fishing. All of these spots highlighted in the figure are within five miles or so of land-- which in some cases is the mainland and in other cases an island, peninsula, etc.

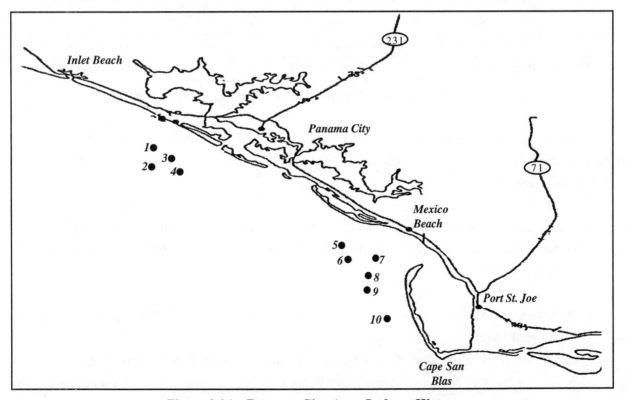

Figure 2.24 - **Panama City Area Inshore Waters**

Spot #	Site Name	LORAN coordinates	Depth (ft)	Structure
1	PCMI Barge Site	14043.8/47000.0	75	Barge, steel objects
2	Warsaw Site	14036.8/46977.2	80	Concrete rubble
	Warsaw Site	14037.2/46977.4	75	Concrete bridge trusses
	Warsaw Site	14031.8/46977.0	75	Concrete bridge deck spans (3)
3	B&B Barge	14087.3/46970.7	42	Barge
	LOSS Pontoon Site	14078.5/46973.8	65	Tires, Scrap steel, Concrete rubble
	LOSS Pontoon Site	14085.4/46874.0	45	Concrete bridge, deck spans (4)
4	Midway Site	14074.5/46946.5	72	Concrete bridge trusses
	Midway Site	14068.8/46949.0	70	Concrete bridge trusses
	Midway Site	14072.4/46949.6	72	Boxcars
	Midway Site	14070.6/46953.1	72	Concrete bridge trusses
	Strength	14076.5/46944.3	75	Minesweeper Tender 'Strength', Boxcar
	Midway Site	14072.6/46949.6	71	Scrap steel, tires, concrete rubble
5	Mexico Beach Site	14116.5/46845.6	55	Boxcars
	Mexico Beach Site	14166.6/46845.5	55	Railroad cars
6	Kaiser	14121.4/46840.6	42	Woodtug "Kaiser"
7	Lumber Ship	14142.9/46830.5	25	Metal ship, framework
8	J.C. Reef	14115.7/46841.1	45	Concrete, auto frames
9	Port St. Joe Reef	14111.6/46802.0	40	Concrete rubble
10	Barrier Dune Barge	14114.9/46741.6	35	200 foot barge

Figure 2.25 - Panama City Inshore Spot Location Coordinates

In addition to the spots highlighted and characterized in Figures 2.24 and 2.25, there are several other Inshore point and area fishing locations you might find interesting. Moving from West to East across the Panama City area, these include the following:

- Around the buoys at the mouth of St. Andrew's Pass. There's usually all kinds of bait around the buoy anchor chains and all kinds of bigger fish partaking of them. The number five buoy has proven particularly productive for Flounder in the Fall.

- Black Bart. A 165 foot long sunken supply ship 5.5 nautical miles Southwest of the Panama City channel in 85 feet of water.

- Buoy Line. A couple of miles offshore from the Mexico Beach canal. Marks the ship channel out of St. Joe Bay into the Gulf. Twenty five to forty feet of water. Troll between the buoys in the Fall for Kings. Cobia hang around the buoys in the Spring.

Given Panama City's substantial number of Bays with their significant access to the Gulf via two Passes, area Inshore fishing is basically a continuation of Bay fishing. Unlike the Destin area farther West, Panama City small boat fishermen can catch many of the Inshore species like Kings and Spanish in the relative comfort of area Bays. Accordingly, there seems to be less emphasis on Inshore fishing as a separate and distinct type of fishing in the Panama City Area. Having said that, it is now time to go Offshore--- which is an important part of the Panama City fishing Story.

Offshore

As noted earlier, Panama City shares the superb big game trolling waters of the Desoto Canyon with both Pensacola and Destin. The other two areas just happen to be a little closer to the action. For example, it's a 30 mile run from Pensacola to the 100 fathom curve. The same curve is roughly 50 miles from Panama City. A description of Desoto Canyon waters was provided in the Pensacola area section. It won't be duplicated here. Instead, the remainder of this section will focus on the other, structure related fishing opportunities available to Panama City area Offshore fishermen.

Figure 2.26 highlights a number of proven Offshore spots that may be of interest to you. Although the map is not to scale, it does provide a relative perspective on the geographical location of deep water sites.

In addition to the spots highlighted in figure 2.27, there are several more offshore points and areas that are worthy of your consideration. They're described below.

- U.S. Army M-60 Tanks

  - Tank #1-West Site   13990.60   46950.60
  - Tank #2-West Site   13990.20   46950.60
  - Tank #3-West Site   13990.40   46950.40
  - Tank #4-West Site   13989.90   46950.50
  - Tank #5-West Site   13990.10   46950.40
  - Tank #6-Center Site   13994.20   46945.00
  - Tank #7-Center Site   13994.30   46945.10
  - Tank #8-Center Site   13994.40   46945.50
  - Tank #9-Center Site   13994.50   46945.60
  - Tank #10-Center site   13994.60   46945.30
  - Tank #11-East Site   13999.60   46940.20
  - Tank #12-East Site   13999.60   46940.10
  - Tank #13-East Site   14000.00   46940.10

- Hathaway Bridge Reef

  - Bridge Truss #1   14070.6/46953.1
  - Bridge Truss #2   14068.8/46949.0
  - Bridge Truss #3   14002.4/46914.3
  - Bridge Truss #4   13997.9/46915.8
  - Bridge Truss #5   14019.3/47031.1
  - Bridge Truss #6   14020.1/47022.8
  - Bridge Truss #7   13949.8/46950.0
  - Bridge Truss #8   13953.8/46955.8
  - Bridge Truss #9   13955.4/46961.0
  - Bridge Truss #10   13952.7/46969.6
  - Bridge Truss #11   14003.8/46790.3
  - Bridge Truss #12   14074.5/46923.3
  - Bridge Truss #13   13995.2/64923.3
  - Bridge Truss #14   14037.2/46977.4
  - Bridge Deck #15   14037.2/47030.3
  - Bridge Deck #16   14031.8/26977.0
  - Bridge Deck #17   14112.6/46841.1
  - Bridge Deck #18   14002.1/46920.1
  - Bridge Deck #19   14085.4/46974.0

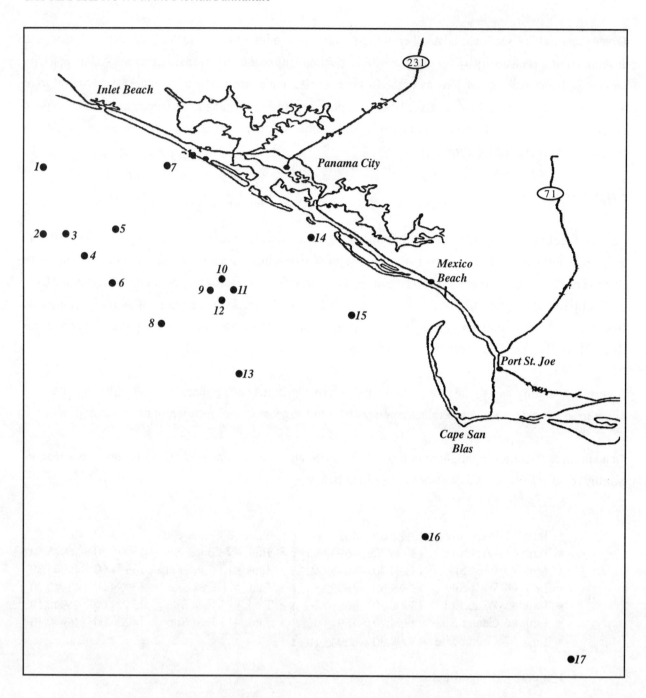

Figure 2.26 - **Panama City Offshore Fishing Spots**

Spot#	Site Name	LORAN Coordinates	Depth (ft.)	Structure
1	Defelix Site	13877.0/47050.0	110	10 fiberglass boat hulls
2	Lang Site	13891.1/46926.0	106	Washers & dryers
	Charles Scott Site 1	13853.5/47022.0		Unknown
3	Siedow's Site	13858.5/47014.0	106	Unknown
4	Grey Ghost	13891.1/46991.7	105	Steel tug, Tires
	Grey Ghost (Blount Reef)	13890.0/46990.0	105	Fiberglass boat parts, tires, steel
	Grey Ghost (Archer Reef)	13891.1/46991.7	105	Bundled tires
5	Hilpert's Site 2	13900.0/47017.0	97	Unknown
6	Hilpert's Site 1	13902.5/46959.2	99	Unknown
7	Fountainbleau Site	14020.1/47022.8	73	Concrete Bridge Trusses
	Fountainbleau Site	14019.3/47031.1	73	Concrete Bridge Trusses
	Fountainbleau Site	14019.8/47028.2	75	Boxcars
	Fountainbleau Site	14019.8/47028.2	72	Concrete Rubble
	Fountainbleau Site	14025.2/47030.3	68	Concrete Bridge Deck Spans (3)
8	Charles Scott Site 2	13950.0/46910.0	110	Tire Modules
9	Stage 1 East	14002.1/46910.2	96	Concrete Bridge Deck Spans
	Stage 1 East	14002.4/46914.3	105	Concrete Bridge Trusses
	Stage 1 West	13953.8/46955.8	115	Concrete Bridge Trusses
	Stage 1 East	13997.9/46915.8	105	Concrete Bridge Trusses
	Pitts Site	14011.3/46925.5	90	Tire Grids
10	Stage 1 West	13852.7/46969.6	115	Concrete Bridge Trusses
	Stage 1 West	13955.4/46961.0	115	Concrete Bridge Trusses
	Stage 1 West	13949.8/46950.0	115	Concrete Bridge Trusses
	Stage 1 East	13995.2/46923.3	105	Concrete Bridge Trusses
	Stage 1 Site	14011.3/46925.5	100	Concrete Rubble
	Chippewa	14012.3/46921.2	96	210 ft. Tugboat "Chippewa"
	Stage 1 East	14011.5/46925.5	95	Boxcars
11	Wm. Dick's Site	14013.0/46926.0	100	Fiberglass Boat hulls
12	M.T. Kelly Site	14005.0/46925.0	100	Tire Bundles
13	J.R. Fuller Site	13961.0/46842.0	110	Autos, tires, appliances
14	Liberty Ship	14065.1/46918.6	72	"Benjamin H. Grierson"
15	Gatewood Barge Reef	14071.0/46823.0	80	70 ft barge, steel tanks, tires, railroad car
16	Brahier Site	13918.2/46909.1	120	Fiberglass boat hulls, tires
17	Empire Mica	14023.4/46489.6	110	465 ft tanker "Empire Mica"

Figure 2.27 - **Panama City Offshore Spot Location Coordinates**

On a concluding note about the Panama City area, there is one more important fact that should be acknowledged. Specifically, and by virtue of **Panhandle** geography, area fisherman get to enjoy what amounts to two different worlds of fishing. The first world is the immediate Panama City area, which is neatly partitioned into the same classical pattern as that found in the Destin and Pensacola areas farther West (ie Bays, Surf, Piers, Inshore, and Offshore). But, without having to travel any significant distance these same fishermen can also enjoy a second world which is inherent in and a part of the Forgotten Coast of the Florida **Panhandle**. We'll take a look at the unique features, challenges and fishing opportunities offered in this stretch of coast in the next section.

—PERSONAL   NOTES—

THE FORGOTTEN COAST

The final segment of what we are calling the Florida ***Panhandle*** stretches from Mexico Beach in the West to Steinhatchee in the East. A portion of this segment also has a name--the Forgotten Coast. According to the local Chambers of Commerce, that is what they like to call the coast from Mexico Beach to Shellpoint/Panacea. For our purposes here, however, a tiny bit of literary license has been exercised. The Forgotten Coast has been extended to include another 75 miles or so of coastline to Steinhatchee because it shares common topography and offers the same kind of extraordinary fishing opportunities.

The Forgotten Coast is unique in Florida waters because it is almost estuarial in nature--even many miles offshore. It includes a significant number of shallow bays, capes, passes, islands, sounds, and lots of rivers. With the possible exception of the seaward side of St. George Island and a couple of other limited stretches, it essentially has no surf in the traditional sense. What much of it does have, however, is endless salt marsh woven with miles of tidal creeks emptying into shallow grass flats laced with limestone outcroppings and oyster bars. Near shore waters deepen very gradually, about one to two feet per mile, as you move farther offshore. By any standard, the results are some very interesting fishing, boating and navigation challenges. Figure 2.28 provides a birds-eye view of the Forgotten Coast.

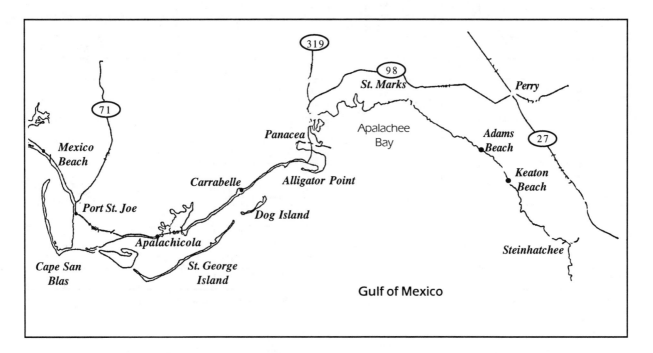

Figure 2.28 - **The Forgotten Coast**

Figure 2.29 reflects the same kind of catch data presented in the three previous sections. The data, however, is only for the Forgotten Coast. It was synthesized from a variety of publications that cover Forgotten Coast fishing. Recall, blanks don't mean the species isn't around--just that no one reported catching some.

Panhandle Gamefish	Historic Monthly Activity											
	J	F	M	A	M	J	J	A	S	O	N	D
Amberjack	X	X	XX	XX	XX	X	X	XX	X	X	X	X
Black Drum	X	XXX	X	X	X	X	X	X	X	XX	XX	X
Black Sea Bass	X	X	X	XX	XX	XX	X	X	X	X	X	X
Blackfin Tuna							X					
Bluefish	X	X	X	XX	XX	XX	XXX	X	X	X	X	X
Blue Marlin												
Bonito			X	X	X							
Cobia			X	XX	XXX	XXX	XX	X	XX			
Dolphin						X	XX	XX	X	X		
Flounder	X	X	XX	XX	XX	XX	XX	XX	XXX	XXX	XX	XX
Grouper	X	X	X	XX	XX	XX	XX	X	XX	XX	X	X
Jack Cravalle				X	X	XX	XXX	XX	X	X	X	
King Mackerel				X	X	XX	XX	X	XX	XX	X	
Northern Mackerel												
Pompano			X	X	X	X	X	X	X	X		
Redfish	X	X	X	XX	XX	XXX	XXX	XXX	XX	XX	XX	X
Sailfish								X	X			
Sheepshead	XX	XX	X	X	X	X	X	X	X	XX	XX	XX
Snapper	X	X	X	X	X	X	X	X	X	X	X	X
Spanish Mackerel			X	X	XXX	XXX	XX	XX	X	X		
Swordfish												
Tarpon				X	XXX	XX	X	X				
Triggerfish				X	X	X	X	X	X	X	X	
Tripletail				X	XX	XX	XX					
Trout	X	X	X	XX	XXX	XX	XX	XX	XXX	XX	XX	X
Wahoo							X	X	X	XX		
White Marlin									X			
Whiting	X	X	XX	X	X	X	X	X	X	X	X	X
Yellowfin Tuna												

Legend: Blank= No reported activity   XX= Good catches reported during the month

X= At least a few reported caught in the area during the month   XXX= Great. Even if you just do a few things right, you're going to catch fish

Figure 2.29 - **Forgotten Coast Annual Fishing Summary**

The monthly fishing activity highlighted above has necessarily been generalized. But, based on historical experience, it does suggest reasonable expectations for any given kind of fish in any given month. The following narrative, developed from first hand reports from bait shops, landings, etc., will sharpen up our focus. The locations identified in the narrative will be highlighted in the sections that follow.

January

- AJ's on the "Zina" wreck off Mexico Beach.
- ACMI TIS Towers off Mexico Beach and Apalachicola good for Grouper, Amberjack and Flounder.
- Sheepshead around the seawall and at Bob Sikes Cut on St. George Island.

February

- Specs and Reds in tidal creeks and deep holes in St. Marks, Wakulla, Ochlochonee, Carrabelle and Steinhatchee Rivers.
- Sea Bass at the mouth of the St. Marks River.
- Sheepshead on the reefs off Steinhatchee.
- Flounder in the St. George Island surf and at Bob Sikes Cut.

March

- Pompano beginning to show along the beaches of St. George Island and Cape San Blas. Lots of Whiting too.
- Good Red Snapper fishing 8-12 miles South-Southeast of Bob Sikes Cut.
- First schools of Spanish on deeper grass flats between St. Marks and Aucilla Rivers.
- Kings starting to show on the three OAR Wakulla Reefs in 50 feet of water.
- Flounder in the Bob Sikes Cut.

April

- Grouper, Snapper, and AJ's on shallow water structure off Mexico Beach.
- Reds, Specs, Flounder, Spanish, Black Sea Bass, Cobia, and Tarpon starting to get aggressive on the grass flats off Keaton Beach and Steinhatchee.
- Around St. George Island, Pompano, Spanish, Specs, Flounder, Reds, Ladyfish, Whiting, Bluefish, and Cobia available.

May

- Great Cobia fishing in the Cape San Blas and St. Joe Bay areas. Dog Island Reef is productive as well as buoys 28, 26 and 24.
- Spanish schooling on the flats off St. Marks, Alligator Point, and Cape San Blas.
- Tripletail around markers in Apalachicola Bay.
- On St. George Island, everything is biting including Tarpon and Tripletail.

June

- Good shark fishing in the "Shark Hole" inside the point of St. Joe Peninsula and the mouth of the Carrabelle River.
- Tarpon starting to show on the flats at St. Marks.
- Grass flats off Steinhatchee producing superior drift fishing for Specs and about 12 other species.
- Big Redfish are the hot target on St. George Island. Try along the seawalls, Sikes Cut, in the Surf, around oyster bars, and at the East end of the island.

July

- Bluefish to 15 pounds in the Surf at St. George and Dog Islands and in the Bob Sikes Cut.
- Specs, Reds, and Flounder in Apalachicola Bay and St. George Island Surf.

- Grouper available 20-35 miles off Keaton Beach on natural bottom structure.
- Sand Trout thick on the area called the "Hump", located West of the main Steinhatchee River channel near offshore marker #18.
- Kings, Spanish, Schoolie Dolphin, and a few Wahoo off Mexico Beach.

August
- Cobia moving East along the buoy line wrecks off Mexico Beach and the beaches along St. Joe Peninsula.
- Amberjack on the "Empire Mica".
- Specs and Reds around the Bob Sikes Cut.
- Tarpon in West Pass between St. Vincent and St. George Islands.
- Tarpon to 150 pounds, Cobia and King Mackerel to 35 pounds in Alligator Harbor.
- Wahoo, White Marlin, Sailfish, and Blackfin Tuna Offshore on the "Swanson" "Madison", and "Johnny Walker" coral domes.
- Specs and Reds off Steinhatchee early and late. Best spots: Just South of the main river channel on the spotty bottom near Pepperfish Keys and on the grass flats near Dallus Creek and Long Grassy Point.
- Grouper and Bull Dolphin Offshore from Carrabelle.

September
- Prime Flounder action in St. Joe Bay, St. Vincent's Sound, between St. George and Dog Islands, and in the Ochlockonee River.
- Specs and Reds chasing white shrimp in Apalachicola Bay.
- Pompano at the East end of St. George Island and in the Bob Sikes Cut.
- Spanish at Markers 16 and 18 off Steinhatchee.
- Kings on the JC and car body reefs and along the buoy line off Mexico Beach.
- Grouper in 40-60 feet of water.
- Specs and Reds on the oyster bars on the back side of St. Vincent Island.
- Specs on the East Flats out of St. Marks.

October
- Reds on the oyster bars in the St. Marks and adjacent East Rivers, West Goose Creek, and the mouth of Rattlesnake Cove on St. George Island.
- King Mackerel on Inshore structure and off Dog Island in 30-40 feet of water.
- Schoolie Dolphin on the buoy line off Mexico Beach.
- Very big Specs and Reds on the flats at the mouth of the Steinhatchee River. Sheepshead starting to show on area reefs.

November
- Apalachicola Bay still full of shrimp. Specs, Reds, Jack Cravalle and Spanish still eating them.
- Some Grouper on the "Rockpiles" around Dog Island.
- Kings along the buoy line and on the car body reefs off Mexico Beach.
- Flounders on the reefs of Steinhatchee.
- Very big Black Drum feeding aggressively around St. George Island.

December

- Specs and Reds in deep holes in spring fed rivers and creeks.
- Sheepshead around pilings and along causeways in Apalachicola Bay.
- Some Grouper on the rockpiles off Dog Island.
- Sheepshead and Flounder on the reefs off Steinhatchee.

With that overview of what bites when in mind, it is now time to get serious about where to fish. We'll focus primarily on three of the five generic kinds of fishing--Bays, Inshore, and Offshore--because that's where the action is on the Forgotten Coast. Surf fishing, per se, will be incorporated into the discussion of area Bay opportunities. Pier fishing will not be covered, since Mexico Beach's very short structure is about all there is in the area.

Bays

Fishing the bays of the Forgotten Coast is, in many respects, a story of grass flats, oyster bars, limestone formations, rocks, rivers, and creeks. Given the sheer size of the area of interest, Figure 2.30 just barely begins to suggest spots where these things play an important role. But, the indicated locations will get you started-- and will help you **CATCH FISH NOW!** in the bay waters of the Forgotten Coast.

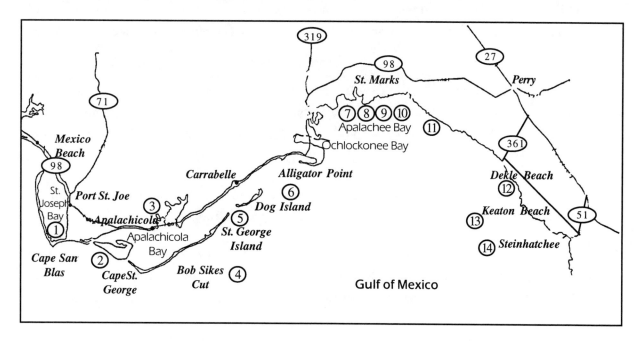

Figure 2.30 - **The Bays and Adjacent Waters of the Forgotten Coast**

Legend

① St. Joseph Bay. Sixty five square miles of marsh, flats, and islands surrounded by a 17 mile long peninsula. More than two dozen small islands are scattered along the bay's shore. St. Joseph State Park is located midway up the North-South part of the peninsula. Camping, cabins, a boat ramp, and super bay and Gulf fishing are immediately available. Try the South end of Black's Island or the shoreline South of the State Park Marina for superior Spec fishing. In cold weather, similarly good Spec fishing is often available off the Port St. Joe Paper Co. oil docks on the East side of the complex. There's a public boat ramp about a mile farther East in the main part of town.

② St. Vincent Island. The island is a 17,000 acre National Wildlife Refuge and the waters around it offer many fishing possibilities. Here are some you may want to try:

- West Pass- between Cape St. George and St. Vincent Island. Holes to 45 feet.
- Dry Bar- an oyster bar that runs from the Northeast corner of St. Vincent out about a mile, then turns South and runs into Apalachicola Bay. The entire bar is good fishing.
- Apalachicola Bay - almost continuous oyster bars off the North shore of St. Vincent island. There's excellent freshwater fishing on the island too, but that's a different story.

③ Apalachicola. There are two spots to consider fishing in the immediate downtown area. The first is a new public dock that runs along the main river channel almost under the overhead Hwy 98 bridge. The second is a pier on the West side of the marina that is just several hundred yards on down the same road. The pier extends out into Apalachicola Bay. According to the local folks, both the dock and the pier are superior places to fish.

④ Bob Sikes Cut. The waters around and adjacent to the jetties are superb fishing for many species year round. The Cut is about six miles from Apalachicola. LORAN numbers for the Sikes Cut jetties are: 14225.0/46530.0

⑤ St. George Island State Park. Great access to both Gulf surf and Apalachicola Bay fishing. Boat ramp. Rattlesnake Cove on St. George Island and Pilot's Cove on Little St. George are also good areas to check out. The Western end of Dog Island Reef - LORAN: 14391.0/46486.0. Water depths average two to four feet.

⑥ Carrabelle - Dog Island Ferry. Passengers only. Operates year round. It takes about an hour to the island. Round trip ticket is $18. Superior fishing for all species all around the island. Really isolated.

⑦ Slough Island Flats at the mouth of Stoney Bayou in the St. Mark's Wildlife Refuge. Low tide is the best time to start fishing. As the tide comes in, Reds and Specs move to limestone formations. Shoreline of Slough Island right up to grass edges also good. Be careful of the big rocks in the water.

⑧ St. Marks River. The flats at its mouth in Apalachee Bay are excellent fishing. Two good spots in this rock strewn area include Black Rock, which is East of the St. Mark's light, and an area called the Rock Garden.

⑨ St. Mark's National Wildlife Refuge. Admission is $4.00 per car. They're open sunrise to sunset. There are two boat ramps between the main gate and the end of the road at the lighthouse. There are limitless possibilities in this area. Several that may be of interest include the following:

- Stake Line- a series of pilings that mark the outer boundary of the refuge;

- Structure- The entire coastline has drop-offs, oyster bars, points, holes, poles and pilings;
- Lighthouse- the area east of the lighthouse is covered with limestone outcroppings. Many are submerged by high tides but have been marked by fishermen. Others have not. All are super fish attractors. Also, absolutely be sure to try the rock jetty that borders the boat canal and extends out into the bay a couple of hundred yards.
- Goose Creek Bay/Live Oak Point- the area is about 4.5 miles east of the St. Marks lighthouse. Running along the Westside of the Bay is a submerged creek bed known as Goose Creek Channel. The channel is 10-13 feet deeper than the flats around it.

If you're fishing the St. Mark's area, be very alert for underwater obstacles. There are a bunch of them!

⑩ Aucilla River. A remote rocky bottom river that empties into Apalachee Bay at the edge of the St. Mark's National Wildlife Refuge. Depending on the time of the year, fish are either in deep holes up the river or on the flats at its mouth. One good area to try is the four mile stretch of coastline between the Pinhook River and Long Point. Best source of current information is the Aucilla River Store located 12.6 miles East of Newport near the bridge on Highway 98.

⑪ Econfina River. Access is off Highway 98. There is a boat ramp at a small fishing camp at the end of Highway 14 a couple of miles upriver from the Gulf. Highway 14 turns off Highway 98 about four miles East of the Aucilla River Bridge. The section of coastline from the mouth of the Econfina River to the mouth of the Aucilla River is dotted with oyster bars and rocky areas. Many have been marked by fishermen with PVC pipe. Fish the pipes.

⑫ Dekle Beach. Flats several hundred yards off shore and South toward Keaton Beach a couple of miles. Three to four feet of water. Great Spec drift fishing.

⑬ Keaton Beach. Nice public park on the water at the end of the road through town. Good access for wade fishing and around a jetty on the channel. Hagen Cove State public use facility is just South of Keaton Beach off Hwy 361. Dirt road leads to a nice park and launch ramp for small boats.

⑭ Steinhatchee. In the Winter, between four to six miles out from the river mouth and in roughly 12 feet of water, trout are the name of the game. A "Steinhatchee Slam" is possible. A slam includes Speckled, Sand and Silver Sea Trout, which all school up in this area.

Surf

Surf fishing, in a traditional sense, is only available along certain parts of the Forgotten Coast. For our purposes here, a definition of "traditional" includes two key components: 1) You fish from a shore that could be called a beach; and, 2) You cast into the Gulf of Mexico. When that definition is applied to the Forgotten Coast, particular stretches can be identified for surf fishing. From the West to East, they include:

- From the Mexico Beach canal East a few miles until the available water essentially becomes St. Joseph Bay.

- The St. Joseph peninsula and Cape San Blas vicinity.
- The Gulf sides of St. Vincent, Little St. George, St. George, and Dog Islands.
- The Gulf Side of Alligator Point.

Fishing along any or all of these pieces of coastline can be both eventful and immensely productive at any given time. If there has been any kind of storm in or around the Gulf, expect challenging surf conditions and the presence of the always dreaded "mud line". If the weather has been good, be prepared to fish in a big glassy pond-- and deal with the challenge of fish who are not being stimulated to feed. Regardless of surf conditions, standby for surprises. During the course of a year, the Forgotten Coast surf offers a real mixed bag of catch possibilities including Specs, Reds, Flounder, Pompano, Cobia, Spanish, huge Bluefish, Tarpon, Ladyfish, and a whole variety of Sharks. Surf fishing can be a ball on the Forgotten Coast!

Inshore

Inshore fishing along the Forgotten Coast is basically different than farther West in the *Panhandle*. This is largely the result of a lack of artificial structure, relatively shallow water, and the fact that you're really fishing a giant bay rather than the open Gulf of Mexico. However, the abundant presence of natural bottom features more than compensates for the shortage of man-made attractors. This is particularly true once you're East of Cape San Blas. All of the spots highlighted in Figure 2.31 are within approximately five miles of land -- which in some cases is the mainland and in other cases an island, peninsula, etc.

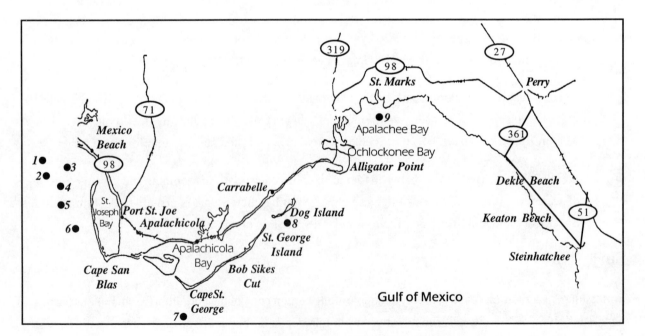

Figure 2.31 - **Forgotten Coast Inshore Waters**

Spot #	Site Name	LORAN coordinates	Depth (ft)	Structure
1	Mexico Beach Site	14116.5/46845.6	55	Boxcars
	Mexico Beach Site	14166.6/46845.5	55	Railroad cars
2	Kaiser	14121.4/46840.6	42	Woodtug "Kaiser"
3	Lumber Ship	14142.9/46830.5	25	Metal ship, framework
4	J.C. Reef	14115.7/46841.1	45	Concrete, auto frames
5	Port St. Joe Reef	14111.6/46802.0	40	Concrete rubble
6	Barrier Dune Barge	14114.9/46741.6	35	200 foot barge
7	L Buoy Reef	14153.9/46536.3	45	Concrete rubble
8	Carrabelle/OAR Reef	14353.4/46475.7	35	Unknown
9	St. Mark's Reef	14478.0/46426.0	20	Concrete culverts

Figure 2.32 - **Forgotten Coast Inshore Spot Location Coordinates**

In addition to these spots, there are several others along the Forgotten Coast you may want to check out. They include the following:

- Wakulla and Taylor County Artificial Reefs. Each reef is constructed of six separate piles of concrete cubes forming a hexagon. Each pile consists of either four or sixteen cubes. Each cube is about three feet on a side and contains one large and four smaller holes. Wakulla #1 - 14474.7/46402.3, Wakulla #2 - 14473.7/46405.6, Taylor #1 - 14471.5/46108.9, Taylor #2 - 14470.3/46109.2

- Buoy Line. A couple of miles Offshore from the Mexico Beach Canal. Marks the ship channel out of St. Joe into the Gulf. Twenty five to forty feet of water. Troll between the buoys in the Fall. Kings. Cobia around the buoys in the Spring.

- Between the Capes. The area between Cape St. George and Cape San Blas. Hard coral bottom. Relatively light fishing pressure. Good for Snapper.

- Apalachicola Bay channel markers. Tripletail. Twelve to fifteen feet of water. Sight fishing.

- East of St. George Island. Bottom is much more rocky than farther West. Good Grouper opportunities for the small boat fisherman.

- Dog Island Area. Good for small boat fishing. Water gets deep within a few miles of the shore. Bottom covered with small rock and reef patches perfect for Grouper.

- Dog Island Reef. Extends from just past Alligator Point to Dog Island. It's about ten miles long and is basically a series of wide sandbars. LORAN numbers for its Western end are: 14391.0/46486.0

- 75 foot steel shrimp boat. Five miles South of the East end of Dog Island. Seventy five feet of water. 14331.4/46470.0

- One More Time Reef. A seventy-five foot shrimp boat sunk on a crashed F-4 fighter. Five miles South of Carabelle Reef in 70 feet of water. 14313.5/46364.6

- Mud Cove. Gulf side of Alligator Point. Tarpon follow bait into the cove in June. The cove is also good for Specs, Spanish, Jack Cravalle and Cobia.

- St. Mark's River Mouth. Sea Bass during the Winter within sight of the lighthouse in 15 feet of water. From about 18 feet of water (Ochlockonee Reef) on out to forty-two feet (20 miles), expect legal Grouper between November and March. Use swimming plugs on downriggers over good looking natural bottom structure.

- Off Steinhatchee. Fish "Seahorse Reef", "Spotty Bottom" and deep grassbeds. Nice Grouper are available about 10 miles off Keaton Beach using big silver and blue Bomber lures on downriggers in twenty to twenty-five feet of water.

Offshore

The following map highlights a number of proven, in many cases year-round, Offshore spots that may be of interest to you. Although the map is not to scale, it does provide a relative perspective on the geographical location of Forgotten Coast deep water sites.

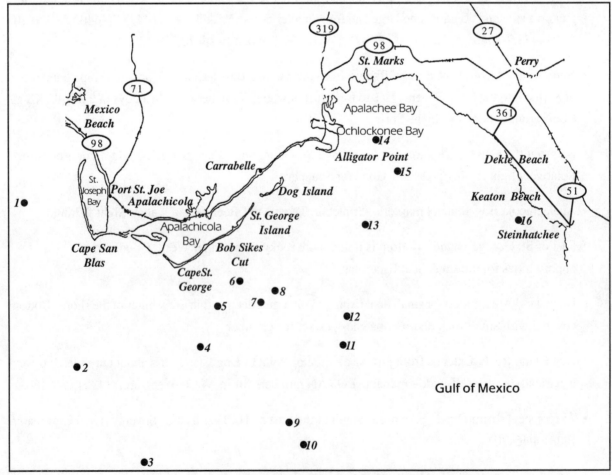

Figure 2.33 - **Forgotten Coast Offshore Waters**

Spot #	Site Name	LORAN coordinates	Depth (ft)	Structure
1	Gatewood Barge Reef	14071.0/46823.0	80	70 ft barge, steel tanks, tires, rroad car
2	Brahier Site	13918.2/46909.1	120	Fiberglass boat hulls, tires
3	Empire Mica	14023.4/46489.6	110	465 ft tanker "Empire Mica"
4	C Tower	14198.2/46393.7	85	Barge, concrete
5	Apalachicola Reef	14217.0/46414.0	75	Bridge material
6	Franklin Co. Reef	14256.0/46431.3	75	Bridge material
7	Carrabelle Reef	14286.8/46379.7	70	Concrete rubble, storage tanks
	Carrabelle Reef	14287.0/46374.8	70	Metal Barge
8	O Tower	14288.4/46376.2	70	Barge, concrete
9	Exxon Reef	14226.9/46246.7	105	Dismantled oil rigs
10	S Tower	14227.8/46245.3	105	Barge, concrete
11	V Tower	14310.4/46202.9	70	Barge, concrete
12	K Tower	14368.0/46346.6	60	Barge, concrete
13	Wakulla OAR Reef Drop 2	14393.6/46353.4	50	Bridge rubble, 34 Boat Molds
	Wakulla OAR Reef Drop 3	14397.5/46346.8	50-55	No material at press time
	Wakulla OAR Reef Drop 1	14394.6/46350.0	54	115 Concrete culverts, 10 steel mixing drums
14	Ochlockonee Reef (Rotary)	14450.6/46422.6	21-30	Concrete, tires
	Ochlockonee Reef (Rotary)	14450.7/46422.5	21-30	Concrete culverts
	Ochlockonee Reef (Rotary)	14449.2/46421.0	30	Concrete culverts
	Ochlockonee Reef (Rotary)	14449.3/46421.0	21-30	Concrete culverts
	Ochlockonee Reef (Rotary)	14449.4/46421.0	30	DC-3 fuselage (10-60')
	Ochlockonee (Rotary)	14450.3/46421.0	21-30	Concrete culverts
15	Barge	14441.3/46346.1	35	Steel barge
16	Steinhatchee Reef	14459.7/46011.3	21	Boat molds, concrete rubble
	Steinhatchee Reef	14460.6/46011.6	20	Metal, concrete
		14458.3/46011.0		Concrete culverts

Figure 2.34 - **Forgotten Coast Offshore Spot Location Coordinates**

In addition to the spots identified and characterized above, there are several more offshore points and areas that may be of interest to you. They're described below.

- Car Bodies. This three to four square mile area is located about seven miles offshore. Its bottom is comprised of both natural and artificial structure. A good LORAN number for the center of the area is 14116.9/46845.6

- Eye of Mexico. This is an area of rocky bottom that's on a heading of 165 degrees from the number one sea buoy at the mouth of the St. Marks River. Thirty five to thirty seven feet of water. Approximate LORAN numbers are 14425 and 46240.

- Gilmer. A dredge boat in seventy eight feet of water. 14160.5/46369.6.

- Yamaha Reef. A two hundred foot hopper barge in seventy five feet of water. 14313.6/46364.8.

- Air Combat Maneuvering Instrumentation (ACMI) Tracking Instrumented Subsystem (TIS) towers. LORAN numbers for these were provided in the previous figure. However, a bit more description may be of interest. The towers are ten story tall steel structures that are anchored in place. There are five towers (K, O, S, V and C) spaced fifteen miles apart in a semicircle, with the "O" tower in the middle. The "O" tower is fifteen miles south of the East Pass between St. George and Dog Islands. The "S" tower is another fifteen miles south and is the farthest offshore of the five towers. The "S" tower is a great spot for Snapper, Grouper, AJ, Blackfin and Yellowfin Tuna, and Triggers, year round. The other four towers are best in the Spring and Fall. The ACMI TIS towers are used to track and evaluate Air Force jet fighters as they engage in mock combat.

- New "Buckeye Reef." The reef is in 47 feet of water, 17.6 miles South-Southwest from marker #1 at Keaton Beach. Over 100 tons of various materials went on the spot in June, 1996.

- Coral Bottoms/Depth Breaks. Coral bottom (Grouper and Snapper) can be found in one hundred forty feet of water off Mexico Beach, ninety feet off Appalachicola, and sixty feet off Carrabelle. Along this same stretch of water, the first depth break of Mexico Beach is thirty two miles at one hundred thirty two feet. The next contour is at thirty five miles and one hundred ninety five feet. The four hundred foot contour is approximately forty four miles off shore.

OK, that's about enough on where and when to fish in **Panhandle** waters. We have covered a lot of territory:
- Over 100 miles of potentially fishable surf.
- Thirteen bays with adjacent bayous, inlets and coves.
- Many river deltas, connecting creeks and passes to the Gulf.
- An abundance of capes, islands, flats, bridges, piers, channels and structure.
- Superb inshore and offshore natural and man-made spots and areas in the Gulf of Mexico.

Our work so far, however, is meaningless-unless we are ready to **CATCH FISH NOW!** We will talk about that in the next chapter.

— PERSONAL NOTES —

CHAPTER 3

HOW TO CATCH FISH NOW!

This chapter will present a detailed discussion of the nearly 30 or so kinds of gamefish waiting for you in *Panhandle* waters. We will look at their physical characteristics and appearance first, and then address proven ways to catch them. The chapter will conclude with a look at the kinds of bait and tackle usually used in the *Panhandle* area.

Amberjack

The Amberjack (AJ) is a relative long, slender fish with the pronounced V tail typical to members of the Jack family. The upper part of his body is dark, either brownish, olive, or steely-blue. The lower part of his body is lighter, with lavender and golden tints. He may also have an amber band from eye to tail.

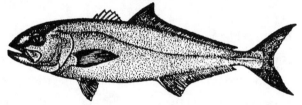

Although small Amberjack of less than legal size (28 inches to the fork) are frequently caught Inshore, legal fish are out in deeper water around structure. In this area, fish to 75 lbs or so can be caught over structure using three different approaches. First, try live bait. The Amberjack will happily consume Mullet, Grunts, Pinfish, or what have you. Use a heavy duty fish finder rig consisting of a 3 to 8 oz egg sinker running free on your line, a 100 lb test barrel swivel, a 3 ft piece of 80 lb test mono, and a 5/0 single bronze hook. Lower your bait down about three fourths of the way to the bottom...and hold on! Second, you can cast a variety of lures. Very large grubs, twister tails, and jigs fished close to the bottom seem to work well. Finally, you can slow troll the area around and over the structure, using either live bait on downriggers or deep diving plugs.

The Amberjack has an intense curiosity and very little fear of man. When you hook one, more than likely the entire school will follow the fighting fish right up to the boat. The other fish will hit new baits tossed to them, and will continue to do so as long as one struggling fish remains in the water. The Amberjack is great eating. The Florida record for Amberjack is 142 pounds.

Black Drum

The Black Drum has a short, deep body with a high-arched back. Its mouth is low and horizontal with the upper jaw projecting beyond the lower. In life, the Black Drum's body is silvery with a brassy sheen, which turns to dark grey after death. Its fins are blackish in color. Unlike its cousin the Redfish, it does not have a black spot at the base of its tail. Black Drum have been caught in this area to over 50 lbs. Black Drum of 10 pounds or less are great eating. Fish larger than that should be released.

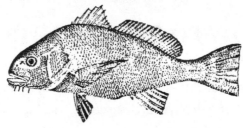

Since the Black Drum is exclusively a bottom feeder, a fish finder rig is the way to go. Thirty pound test mono should be used for your leader with a 2/0 to 4/0 bait holder hook.

Bait for the Black Drum is not very exotic. As a bottom feeder, he will take about anything you put down including clams, oysters, mussels, crabs, and particularly, live or fresh dead shrimp. The Florida record for Black Drum is 93 pounds.

Black Sea Bass

This tasty eating fish is dark brown or black in color with a dorsal fin that has rows and stripes of white on black. Large males have iridescent blue and ebony marking and a fatty hump just in front of their dorsal fins. There is usually a blue pattern around the eyes of both the male and female. Black Sea Bass are common to about a pound and a half (13 inches) and the Florida record for this guy is five pounds, one ounce.

Black Sea Bass can usually be found in area bays and bayous and in Inshore waters. The can be trolled for using a small planer and a spoon or bottom fished using almost any color small jig, plastic grub, or twister trail. Given the aggressiveness of this fish, tandem rigs are particularly effective. Just tie a three-way swivel to the end of your line and two different length leaders to the other two swivel eyes. Finish the rig off with a couple of jigs of your choosing. An egg sinker above the swivel may be necessary to stay close to the bottom if you're in deeper waters. A small squid strip on each jig enhances the chances of regular "doubles". Work your bait slowly, in short hops, for the best results. Natural offerings include small live minnows and cut bait.

Blackfin Tuna

This member of the Mackerel family is one of the smallest tuna. It has a typical tuna shape with generally dark coloring over its entire body. It has finlets behind the second dorsal and anal fins which are uniformly black, hence its name. Blackfins in this area may reach 35 lb, but most are less than 10 lbs. Regardless of size, they are delicious eating.

Probably the most effective way to catch Blackfins Inshore is either drifting or slow trolling live bait. The rig for them is simple. Tie a barrel swivel to the end of your line. Then tie on a 3 ft piece of 50 lb test mono with a 2/0 or so treble hook. Although you're going to lose a few rigs and baits if sharp-toothed King Mackerel are in the area, mono is still the way to go! Blackfin are very shy of wire leaders. Vary the depth you are fishing with different sized rubber core sinkers attached to your line above the swivel. Pinfish are probably the best bait, but Blackfins will also take Grunts, small Mullets, Alewife, and Cigar Minnows.

Offshore, if you are in an area where Blackfin have been reported, go fast! Pull rigged Ballyhoo at sufficient speed to skip them along the surface. This approach is a proven tuna-getter. Lures are also used effectively for Blackfin Offshore. Clark Spoons, Softheads in a variety of colors, and California and No Alibi feathers have all worked well. They should be pulled 100-300 feet behind the boat. If no surface action develops, run your lures deep behind a #2 or #3 planer.

Bluefish

At various times, this popular game fish may be found along all area beaches, around jetties, off piers, and over natural structure in area bays. It has a moderately stout body and a belly that is flat sided but blunt edged on the ventral surface. The Bluefish has a slightly pointed snout and a large oblique mouth with a projecting lower jaw. It has prominent, very sharp canine teeth. Its coloration is generally blue-green above, shading to silvery-white on the belly. Bluefish in this area range in size from 7-9 inch "snappers" to 20 pound plus "monsters". Regardless of size, they have a well earned reputation for savagery when on a feeding rampage, maiming or killing everything in their path including their own kind. Never put your fingers in a Bluefish' mouth, no matter how dead he may appear!

There are two basic ways to catch Bluefish. Each can be effective under a variety of conditions. Sometimes both can be used interchangeably as described below. If Bluefish are known to be working an area surf, bait fishing is always a good approach. During the day, chunks of cut bait fished on the bottom using a two-hook spreader or fish-finder rig can be productive. Cut Mullet has consistently proven to be the best bait followed closely by cut Cigar Minnows. Heavy wire two hook spreaders (which can be purchased at any tackle store) should be configured with a one to three ounce pyramid sinker on the bottom, 1/0 or 2/0 hooks attached directly to the two spreaders clips, with your line tied to the barrel swivel at the top. If you're surf fishing, your rig should be cast out as far as possible, preferably beyond the second bar.

A fish finder rig is an effective alternative to a two-hook spreader and allows your bait to move around the area you are fishing. It is nothing more than an egg sinker (again, one to three ounces) sliding freely on your line, which is tied to one side of a barrel swivel. Up to 30 inches of wire leader with a 1/0 or 2/0 hook is attached to the other side of the barrel swivel. Plastic coated, store bought leaders are okay for Bluefish but just don't work for the Kingfish we'll talk about later.

Whole frozen Cigar Minnows or live bait such as Pinfish, fingerling Mullet, or Bull Minnows are another deadly approach to catching Bluefish. During the day, a fish finder rig like that described above except with a 2/0 treble hook can be used effectively. Use of a partially water-filled large clear casting float instead of an egg sinker should also be tried. It will give you the weight you need for long distance casts and will keep your bait up off the bottom for easier visibility. Regardless of whether you are fishing a sinker or a float, your bait should be hooked as follows: Cigar Minnows, once through the eye socket; fingerling Mullet and Bull Minnows, through both lips; and Pinfish, just under the skin crosswise in front of the dorsal fin.

Night fishing for the really big Blues is also popular and potentially productive. Fish weighing up to 20 pounds have been successfully landed in the ***Panhandle*** area. The approach and rig, in this case, is simple. Tie your line to a barrel swivel to which a 20-30 inch steel leader with a 3/0 treble hook attached. Hook on a whole Cigar Minnow, cast out as far as possible, and hold on! The Florida record for Bluefish is 22 pounds, three ounces.

Every few years, for no known reason, giant Bluefish invade some Panhandle waters in the Springtime. Several locations so blessed have included: the sea buoy off Destin's East Pass; Cape San Blas; Bob Sikes Cut; and, the surf on St. George and Dog Islands. Unfortunately, nobody knows when and where the jumbo Blues will make their next appearance.

Blue Marlin

The Blue Marlin is the largest of the Atlantic Marlin family. It is common to 11 feet in length and is known to exceed 2000 pounds in weight. All trophy size fish are females because males seldom grow much over 300 pounds. A Blue Marlin is good to eat.

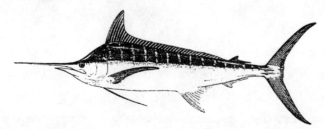

Both rigged natural baits and a variety of lures can be effective in Offshore Desoto Canyon waters. Choosing between the two, however, often comes down to a question of speed. Specifically, because the Canyon area hotspots are separated by substantial distances, a brisk (minimum of 8-9 knots) trolling speed is required to cover as much potentially productive water as possible. Natural baits just do not hold up long or well moving this fast or faster.

The choice of lures usually focuses on flat or slant-face plastics in medium and large sizes. Some other observations by ***Panhandle*** Offshore experts provide additional useful insights.

- Lure size - One school of thought says big only. Softhead, C&H or Snider lures rigged with 12/0 or 14/0 Mustad hooks or regular steel are preferred. Another school says think small. Lures with short heads, measuring no more than seven to twelve inches including skirt, are considered the best. Popular head styles are those that produce plenty of splash and smoke (bubbles), even at moderate trolling speeds. Using this approach, Reto's Rigs, Boone's Airheads, R&S small Teardrops with their skirts trimmed, standard softhead Hookers, and rubber squids are all lures that have worked well in the Desoto Canyon area.

- Lure Color - There has been much debate about the ability of fish to see color. Two basic principles work well. Dark colors can be seen as a silhouette against the mirror-like ocean surface by a fish rising from deep below the bait. Light colors can be seen by a fish swimming on the surface and viewing the lure against the dark blue ocean background. Of course, you can also choose to imitate the color of the baitfish that may be present. Try blue and silver to simulate flying fish, or green and yellow to mimic Dolphin.

- Live Bait - Great approach if Blues are known to be in the area. A trolling speed of 1-2 knots is about right. Good baits include: Black Jacks, Goggle Eyes, Big Eye Scads, Blackfin Tuna, Bonito, and small Yellowfin Tuna. When Yellowfin are schooling on the surface, catch one, put him down 50 feet or so on a downrigger--- and hold on!

- Lure Spread - One popular trolling spread consists of five lures, two on flatlines, two from outriggers, and one shotgun down the center. The darkest bait is run on the shotgun about 250 feet behind the long rigger, at about the fifth wave behind the transom. The close flatline is usually the largest lure in the spread and is often in a lighter color.

- One Effective Trolling Pattern - In the early morning (sunup) and starting at the East end of the Spur, fish toward Desoto Canyon. Keep the sun at your back as much as possible. Its tough to see your baits looking back into the sun, but its easier for the fish to see the baits with the sun behind them. Don't troll in a straight line because a school of bait doesn't move that way. Tack back and forth. By noon, be near the East wall of the Canyon (13350/46750). Fish toward the Canyon Cap at 13300 and 46785. Throughout the day, whenever you are over significant bottom structure like peaks or channels, work each area thoroughly. The real Pro's like to use a search pattern in the shape of a box. Get a Loran fix over the prominent under water structure. Then use the fix as the center of a box and run North and South 5-20 minutes until your boat has covered each side of the box three times. Do the same thing running East and West. If the fish are deep, it may take several passes to get their attention.

So, the bottom line on *Panhandle* Blue Marlin? Simple. They are out there and they are big. The Florida record fish of 980 pounds came from the Desoto Canyon area!

Bonito

The Bonito is a mackerel-shaped fish that is a blueish-steel color on the upper body, shading off to silvery sides and a white belly. He has dark stripes running diagonally down and forward across his upper body. Bonito average 4 to 15 lbs in this area, and are usually an unwanted byproduct of trolling for King Mackerel.

Although this member of the Mackerel family is usually not eaten in this area, it is a superior bait for catching Sharks and Swordfish. Bonito are a lot of fun to catch on light tackle, will hit on almost anything you throw in the water, and often will oblige -- when nothing else will bite. It is not unusual to see half mile square schools of Bonito in Summertime *Panhandle* waters.

Cobia

From a distance, this fish looks vaguely like a Catfish and/or a Shark. It has a relatively wide, horizontally aligned mouth and a forked tail. Its upper body is dark brown, its sides somewhat lighter, and its belly a very pale brown. Younger fish have a black lateral band extending from their nose across their eyes back to the base of their tails. A Cobia's fins are mostly black. Spring run Cobia average between 20-50 lbs, but fish over 100 lbs are caught each season. Recently, a 137 pound Cobia was caught in *Panhandle* waters. The fish would have been a new world record if the charter boat Captain had not hooked the fish and then passed the rod to his client. Cobia are absolutely delicious eating.

Spring fishing for Cobia during their Westward migration along the *Panhandle* is exciting. Since it is almost exclusively sight fishing, there is a real premium on eyesight, boat handling, and casting precision, An elevated position for fish spotting is a real advantage. Accordingly, almost every kind of tower imaginable (including ladders) get mounted on even the smallest local boats. The secret to effective spotting is to run parallel to the beach but far enough out so that you can look into swells backdropped by the white sand of the outer bar. Dark shapes just under the surface show up well under these conditions. When a shape is spotted, your boat needs to be maneuvered so you can cast far enough ahead of the target that you won't spook it. If in doubt, assume the dark shape is a Cobia and react accordingly.

As with most other Inshore gamefish, Cobia can be taken on both live bait and lures. Preferred baits include Blue Crabs, Pinfish, Eels (if you can find them), Mullet, and large Alewife. Hair or feather jigs, in 1-1/2 oz to 3oz sizes and every conceivable color, are probably the most popular lures. Chartreuse, chartreuse and yellow, purple, and white have been particularly good colors over the years. Pieces of a whole plastic worm hooked on the jig have enhanced fishing success over the last several seasons. A squid head with the tentacles still attached is even better. Tube and Dingaling lures and a variety of artificial eels have also worked well. Regardless of whether you fish live bait or lures, you must use a 30 inch or so piece of 50 lb test mono and a barrel swivel for attachment.

Cobia are powerfully attracted to floating objects of any kind. Accordingly, local fishermen keep a sharp eye out for debris, large Sea Turtles, and Rays. More often than not, there will be at least one and sometimes an entire pod of Cobia under such floating objects.

Sight fishing for Cobia can also be done from ***Panhandle*** area piers. This type of fishing also puts a premium on eyesight and casting distance and accuracy. One to three ounce jigs in every conceivable color are again the preferred lures. They should be tied to a 30 in. piece of 30-50 lb test mono with a black barrel swivel. Chartreuse, white, chartreuse and yellow, and purple have traditionally been hot colors. Many pier fishermen also like to spice up their jigs with plastic worms of all sizes and colors. The actual catching process goes something like this. Fishermen on the pier closely watch the water in all directions. The first person to spot the dark shape of a Cobia approaching the pier calls "first cast". He or she then monitors the progress of the fish into casting range. Pier protocol demands he or she get the first cast. However, if the fish does not take the first offered bait, DUCK! About 9,000 other baits will be in the air within fractions of a second.

Inshore waters along the beach are not the exclusive habitat of ***Panhandle*** Cobia. At many times of the year, Cobia can also be caught around structure in ***Panhandle*** area bays and bayous, and while bottom fishing on Inshore and Offshore structure.

Dolphin

In the water, Dolphin are usually a vivid greenish-blue with dark vertical bands that may appear and disappear. When the fish is hooked, his color fluctuates rapidly between blue, green, and yellow. After death, these colors fade rapidly to a uniform yellowish shade. Dolphin typically have relatively blunt heads and bodies that taper back to a very pronounced fork tail. The Florida record for Dolphin is 77 pounds, 12 ounces, and its fighting ability is legendary. Swimming speeds have been clocked in excess of 50 knots.

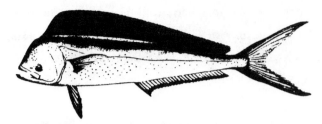

A Dolphin strikes explosively, fights frantically, and performs beautifully in the air. As noted elsewhere, from time to time they congregate by the hundreds or thousands along tide lines or weed lines just a few miles offshore. When this happens, the name of the game is to troll Baby Dusters with squid strips or small feathers along these lines. When hookups occur, stop the boat, break out the light spinning tackle, and start throwing small jigs, spoons, etc. As an aside, make sure you keep one hooked fish in the water at all times. This will help insure that the rest of the school will stick around. Catching two to ten pound schoolie Dolphin on light tackle is never-to-be-forgotten experience. The are absolutely superior fighters with a full bag of acrobatic tricks. They are also superb eating.

Fishing for big Dolphin Offshore is unlike the pursuit of other pelagic species in this area. As others have pointed out, it's more like hunting than fishing. The secret is not blind trolling. Rather, it's a case of high speed running while looking for indications of fish or spots/things that may hold them. Circling Frigate Birds are the best indication, weed lines are good spots, and any kind of flotsam is the kind of thing likely to have Dolphin close by.

Big Dolphin ("Bulls") will hit just about any kind of lure or bait, including those intended for Marlin. Feather jigs, rigged Ballyhoo and strip baits, Moldcraft Hookers, Dolphin Juniors and Seniors, and Jelly bellies all work well for bull and cow Dolphin. Although color doesn't seem to matter all that much, many fishermen swear by greens, yellows, white, and orange/yellow. With regards to natural bait, big live baits are the best. In the **Panhandle** area, Blue Runners are usually the easiest to catch and they are super for big Dolphin. Ten inches or longer is about the right size.

A final suggestion might be of interest. Specifically, and at one time or another, you'll encounter a weed line loaded with schoolie sized Dolphin of a three to five pounds. You were hoping for something bigger. Don't despair. Frequently, much bigger Dolphin are under the shoolies-- which they eat from time to time. If you planned ahead, you'll have a large live Pinfish or Blue Runner on board. Toss it outside the schoolies, hooked so it swims down (behind the dorsal fin). Standby for action!

Flounder

There are a number of different kinds of Flounder in **Panhandle** waters year round. All share some common characteristics. These include a broad, flat body with both eyes on one side of the head. Their bottom sides are generally whitish in color and their top sides (where their eyes are) are grey-brown. Flounder caught in the surf tend to have very light coloration on their top sides to more closely match the white sand bottom they live on. Size ranges between 10-20 inches in length with "doormats" over 25 inches caught occasionally. Flounder are outstanding eating.

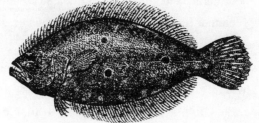

Flounder can be caught almost anywhere except perhaps Offshore using either bait or lures. The preferred approach in bait fishing is a fishfinder rig with a ½ oz to 1 ½ oz egg sinker and 24 inches of 12-15 lb test line as a leader. Small (#2-#4) treble or standard hooks are about right. Small fingerling Mullet, Pinfish, or Croakers, which you have to catch yourself, or Bull Minnows, that can be obtained at a bait shop, are the preferred baits. There are times, however, when other baits such as fresh dead shrimp, sandfleas, cut bait strips, and fiddler crabs will also take Flounder. Live shrimp, of course, is always an effective albeit expensive choice.

Using lures for Flounder can be a lot of fun, particularly on ultra light tackle. In this area, all of the following will catch fish:

- Plastic grubs - white, white with a hot pink tail, chartreuse, dark green with a fire tail, and rootbeer.

- Plastic curly tail jigs - white, chartreuse, dark green with a fire tail, and metal flake clear/grey. Experiment with white, red or chartreuse jig heads with the various tail colors.

- Small (½ oz) gold spoons

- Small jigs - white, yellow, or hot pink skirts

- Small, sinking gold or silver Rapalas or Rebels

One recent particularly effective technique has been a white or hot pink jig sweetened with either a small strip of Flounder belly or small live Bull Minnow.

If you plan to drift the edges of channels with live Bull Minnows, you might want to try the following Flounder rig. Tie a snap swivel on one end of a 2 ft piece of 15-20 lb test mono. Now feed on a small day glow orange bead, a small barrel swivel, and another orange bead, in that order. Then, tie another barrel swivel to the other end of your 24 inches of mono. Finish the rig by tying on another 24 inch piece of mono to the barrel swivel between the beads. Then tie on a 1/0 English bait hook on the end of that. As far as weight goes, use sufficiently heavy bell shaped sinkers to bounce the rig along the bottom. For what it's worth, the real Flounder purists paint their bell shaped sinkers either yellow or orange. They claim it has favorable effect on the fishes' feeding behavior.

In a variation on the theme, another popular way to catch Flounder in the *Panhandle* is with a gig. The usually clear shallow water and sandy bottoms around almost the entire area are ideal for this approach. The scenario goes like this. During the day, Flounder lie off the shore in deeper water. At night, however, they come into the shallows (1-3 feet) to chase minnows. They become visible and vulnerable -- if you happen to be quietly drifting through the area in a shallow draft boat. The only equipment you will need is a gig head mounted on some kind of a handle, and a light source. There are commercially available floating 12V lights or you can make your own with a 12V sealed beam headlight. Flounder are usually available for gigging from early Summer to mid-Fall.

Grouper

Of the 50 or so Grouper species found in Florida waters, about 10 can be caught in the *Panhandle* area. Four of the most common are highlighted below.

The Gag Grouper is brownish grey in color with dark worm-like markings on its sides. Its tail is slightly concave and its anal and caudal fins have a white margin on them. The world record of 71 pounds, 3 ounces for a Gag was set in *Panhandle* waters.

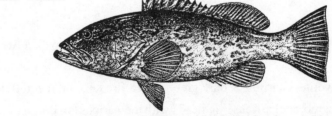

The Black Grouper has olive or grey body coloration with black blotches and brassy spots. Black Grouper are common to 40 pounds and sometimes are caught over 100 pounds. There is no Florida record, however, because this fish is frequently confused with the Gag, which is often mistakenly called a "black grouper".

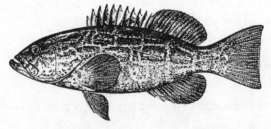

The Red Grouper is a squatty shaped fish that is generally olive-grey in color with a slight salmon cast to it. Its jaws are pale olive with a slight reddish cast to them. It has dark bars on its head and body and, on some fish, there are also scattered white spots. The Florida record for this fish is 39 pounds, 8 ounces.

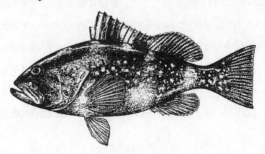

The Scamp, which is an important member of the Grouper family, is generally smaller than either the Black or Gag. It is light grey or brown in color with elongated caudal fin rays. It has reddish-brown spots on its sides that tend to be grouped into lines and frequently there is a little yellow around its mouth. The Florida record for a Scamp is 28 pounds.

Before leaving this introduction, one other Grouper found in Panhandle waters is worthy of mention. His name is Warsaw, and he is one of the largest members of the clan. Proof of that is the current world record, set in **Panhandle** waters, of 436 pounds, 12 ounces.

So, now its time to go Grouper fishing. If you are going to be fishing wrecks and rockpiles in area bays or on structure in Inshore or Offshore waters, a fish finder rig is they way to go. Use a large enough egg sinker to just get your bait on the bottom. A 5/0 hook, six to eight feet of 80 lb mono test leader, and live bait finish the rig. While Grouper will take dead bait like butterflied Mingo Snappers, usually live bait just has more appeal. Live Pinfish, Cigar Minnows, and Herring are routinely used in this area, with the latter being preferred due to its shininess in the water. Grouper usually feed by sight. In St. Andrews Bay, 10 inch or so Pigfish are a Grouper favorite.

When fishing for Grouper in the deeper Offshore waters, you might want to consider using Dacron line. Dacron doesn't stretch the way monofilament does and can be a big help in instantly popping a big fish off the bottom. A good compromise is to use the lower visibility mono for your leader attached to your Dacron line.

Drifting over deep water structure can also be productive, particularly if you've got a downrigger. In this approach, hook a big Pinfish just ahead of the dorsal fin with a 5/0 treble hook. Use a 15 or 20 ft drop back from the downrigger weight. Lower your bait to about five feet above the structure and then bump your boat in and out of gear to just barely maintain forward motion. Other good live baits include Blue Runners and Porgys -- and two pound Jack Cravalles with their tails chopped off if you are looking for giant Warsaws.

Under the right circumstances and at suitable spots, Grouper can also be caught effectively using lures. For fish like the Black Grouper, trolling speeds up to six knots are about right and large, big lipped, plugs get the job done. Deep jiggers rely on drifting and fishing different depths. In this approach, two to four ounce bucktail or plastic tail lead head jigs in a variety of colors can be effective.

Jack Cravalle

The Jack Cravalle has a light olive back, greyish gold sides, and a yellowish belly. He is blunt-nosed and has a broad forked tail. There is a distinct black spot on each of his gill covers. The average weight of a Jack Cravalle is three to five pounds. But, in August and September, schools of 30-40 pound fish frequent large sections of **Panhandle** Bay and Inshore waters. The Florida record for the Jack Cravalle is 51 pounds.

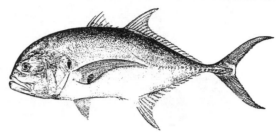

There are two basic ways to catch Jack Cravalle. Live bait fishing using large (7-10 in.) Alewife is always a productive approach. Use a 2 to 3 ft leader of 30-40 lb test mono, a barrel swivel, and a 5/0 to 7/0 hook. The Alewife can be hooked through the nose, the back behind the dorsal fin, or near the anal fin. Although the bait can just be freelined, many folks locally use a float above the leader to help keep track of their lines.

Lures are another effective approach for Jack Cravalle. They will hit almost any kind of top water plug, bucktail jig, plastic grub, or spoon. Surface chuggers probably provide the ultimate in catching excitement for this correctly named "bulldog of the sea".

Regardless of whether you choose bait or lures, your reel should be loaded with at least 200 yards of at least 20 lb test line. Allow about an hour to bring in a 30 pounder and use a net to land the fish. Jack Cravalle are not good eating, so should be released to fight again.

King Mackerel

A King Mackerel is a relatively long, slender fish with a mouth full of very impressive teeth. He has an iridescent bluish green back with shades to silver on his sides and white on his belly. Juvenile Kings frequently have spots on their sides like Spanish Mackerel, but these rapidly disappear as the fish mature. Spring schoolie Kings average 8 to 20 lb. However, later in the season, 30-50 lbs plus is not all that unusual. The Florida King record currently stands at 90 pounds.

King mackerel can be caught in a variety of ways. Probably the single most common is to troll Dusters with frozen Cigar Minnows. A Duster is nothing more than an ounce or so lead head with a hole through it. The head is usually painted white and is most usually trimmed with a 3-5 inch mylar skirt. Although skirts come in a variety of single and multiple colors, green, blue, white and pink prism colors seem to be consistently the best.

A Duster may be rigged in one of two ways. The only difference between the ways is the hook arrangement. In one arrangement, a commercially available "Mino-Troll" rig is used. It provides both a mechanism for attaching a frozen Cigar Minnow to the Duster and a hook for catching fish. A 30 inch piece of 40 lb. test or stronger single strand wire leader is run through the hole in the Duster head and then attached to the Mino-Troll with a haywire twist.

The other way to rig a Duster is to build a Cigar Minnow holder into the leader itself. In this case, your wire goes through the head of the Duster and is haywire twisted onto the eye of a 7/0 conventional or 3/0 treble hook. When you put the wire through the eye of the hook, pull it through far enough so that when the twist is complete, there's about three inches of excess wire remaining. Now, bend that little piece of wire up and away from the twist at a 45-degree angle. Halfway out that piece, bend the remaining inch and a half back down to your leader. Finish the rig by bending a small U shape on the end of the wire. In actual use, the little V shaped wire is pushed up through Cigar Minnow's head, starting under the jaw and existing between the eyes. Pre-poking the hole in the Minnow's head with a nail, ice pick, or awl helps the process considerably. It is then bent down the outside of the minnow's nose and clipped to the leader. It sounds complicated, but it really isn't.

A couple of other thoughts about Dusters and Cigar Minnows might be helpful. First, Kings are notorious for striking short. Accordingly, most fishermen in this area use trailer hooks. To do this, just slightly open the eye of another 7/0 or smaller hook. Now slip the barb of your primary hook through the opened eye and then recrimp it. You now have a trailer hook. A variation on this for treble hooks is equally easy. Attach about 10 inches of wire leader to the eye of your primary hook with a haywire twist. Then, depending on the size Cigar Minnows you have, attach the same size or smaller treble to this piece of wire. Your trailer hook should extend back to about the Minnow's tail. Second, when you start trolling your Duster/Cigar Minnow, you cannot allow it to spin. The minnow must appear to be swimming. If it doesn't, massage and wiggle it to break more bones or smack it against the water for the same reason. You will not catch fish if your bait spins. Finally, Kings will frequently stop feeding on the surface where your Duster is. For whatever reason, they'll go deep and you have to get your Duster down to them. One way to do that is with a planer. Planers come in a number of designs and sizes. Usually a #1 (small) is used for a shallow depth and a #3 for deeper depths. Regardless of the kind or size you decide to use, make sure you tie on at least 10 feet of 50# test mono from the back of the planer to the barrel swivel connection with your wire Duster leader. Obviously, downriggers are a very desirable alternative to planers.

Another way to catch Kings is with lures. Unfortunately, there have been periods over the last several years when this was the only way to fish for them. Cigar Minnows never came in where commercial fishermen could net them. The result was no frozen Minnows available to sweeten Dusters. Having said that, however, lures can and do catch fish. Some of the more popular and successful include Tony Acceta Pet Spoons (#18 and #21), Crippled Alewife Spoons, big Cordell Spots (blue top and silver sides), silver Magnum Rapalas, red and white Cisco Kids, and large blue and silver, jointed, Creek Chub Pikies. This last lure seems to be particularly effective for big Kingfish in the Fall. As was true with Dusters, wire leaders are mandatory and planers should be tried if the fish go deep.

A final way to catch Kings is with live bait. Talk about excitement! First, you have to catch your bait. This is most effectively done with light spinning tackle and bait catcher or similar rigs described in a moment for pier use. Good places to try are around the deep water pilings of bridges, and around the ends of the jetties through area passes. Once bait (Cigar Minnows, Alewife, small Hardtails, etc.) has been caught, you have to keep it alive. This can be in a live well, portable bait tank with recirculating pump or aerator, or in a large trash can with manually recirculated water.

A rig for live bait is simple -- a barrel swivel, a piece of wire leader, and a treble hook sized for the bait you have caught. Hook your bait through the eye socket and troll slowly or just drift. But, before you do that, check directly under your boat. King Mackerel are often similar to Cobia in their fascination with floating objects. Therefore, at the start of, and periodically during your fishing, put a rubber core sinker on your line, and lower your live bait straight down.

There are several similar ways of fishing for Kings off a pier. Perhaps the most popular way is with live bait that you catch yourself. While bait catching techniques vary, three methods are common. The first is with a gold hook rig. This is nothing more than a 4 ft piece of monofilament line with a small sinker tied to one end and three to five #8 to #10 gold hooks tied directly on the line. The rig is lowered into the water around the pier pilings and twitched. Bait fish do the rest, actually biting on the bare gold hooks.

A second way to catch live bait is with a goofy looking thing called an Alewife rig. Available in most area tackle stores, this rig and its operation almost defy description. They are both simple, however. The rig consists of a 2 ft. piece of red yarn with a 4 in. wide piece of monofilament net running its length. A small sinker is on one end and a swivel on the other. To operate the rig, you just lower it into the water, and that's it. The Alewife are apparently curious about the yarn, come to examine it, and become caught in the net.

Snagging is a third and last resort in catching live bait. Tie a small sinker on the end of your line and one or two treble hooks directly to your line. Cast the rig out into visible schools of bait, let it sink a bit, and jerk smartly while retrieving. As an aside, if all three approaches to live bait catching fail, frozen cigar minnows sometimes provide an acceptable alternative.

Once live bait has been caught, it should be transferred immediately to your heavier tackle. A terminal rig consisting of a black #8 or #10 barrel swivel, 24 inches of at least 40 lb test steel leader, and a #2 or larger treble hook should already have been tied on your line. Hook the live bait through the front of its eye socket while carefully avoiding the pupil. Now cast your bait as far as possible away from the pier and hold on to your rod tightly. The fun is about to begin!

Although Kings are a migratory species usually present in **Panhandle** waters in the Spring, Summer and Fall, there are Winter possibilities too. Specifically (and somewhat uniquely), nice Kings can be caught in Panama City's St. Andrews Bay in the January-February period.

A final suggestion on Kings is appropriate. As noted earlier, they have a nasty set of teeth. They also get very cranky after being hooked. So, after you have gaffed your fish but before you turn him loose in the boat or on the pier, hit him very soundly on the top of the head with something substantial. You will be sorry if you don't.

Pompano

The Common Pompano is a wide-sided, relatively narrow fish. Its back and upper sides are grayish-silvery blue and its belly is yellow tinted. Its upper fins are dark in color and its lower fins have a yellowish or light orange cast to them. There is a blue patch just above its eyes, and its yellowish tail is deeply forked. On the average, **Panhandle** Pompano weight between 1-1/2 to 3 lbs. However, fish in the 5-6 lb range have been caught at various spots in the area. There is a bag limit of 10 fish and the minimum size limit is 10 inches. The Florida record for Pompano is eight pounds, one ounce.

Pompano is prized by gourmets as being without peer from either fresh or saltwater. Its flesh is firm and rich. It brings the highest price at the fish market of any fish caught in Florida waters. In addition to superior eating, it is also an outstanding gamefish on light tackle. It strikes hard, runs fast, uses its flat-sided body to execute sudden reversals, and frequently jumps, carrying sinkers and rigs or lures with it. In short, it is a truly world-class fish.

Pompano are the most plentiful in the surf in the Spring and Fall. They run in schools along the beach and tend to move in and out with the tide. Accordingly, one good time to fish for them is usually during the two hours preceding a high tide. Two other good times to fish, regardless of the tide, are at sunup and around sundown. If you can only fish one period during the day, sunup is absolutely the best.

There are two basic approaches to fishing for Pompano in the **Panhandle** area surf. Both, however, rely on a couple of common facts for success. First, Pompano feed on a variety of mollusks and small crustaceans. In this area, that means they primarily eat Sandfleas. Second, they do their Sandflea eating in the troughs between the two sand bars that parallel local beaches. Wave action stirs up the food and the Pompano are there waiting. Given these facts then, it is apparent where to fish using either of the two approaches outlined below.

Baitfishing for Pompano is simple and straightforward. Two popular rigs are the fish finder and the two-hook spreader. A fish finder rig for Pompano is easy to put together. First, cut off a 12-18 inch piece of your line. Set it aside. Now slide a ½ to 3 oz. egg sinker (depending on surf conditions and the weight of your tackle) up your line and then tie the line to one end of a #5 or so black barrel swivel. Next, tie the piece of line you cut off earlier to the other end of the swivel. The fish finder rig is finished off by tying on a hook sized for the Sandfleas you'll be using. Usually a #1 hook is about right. Two-hook spreaders, available at any tackle store, usually come equipped with a barrel swivel at the top end to tie your line to and a snap swivel at the bottom end to attach to your sinker. Pyramid sinkers of 1 oz to 3 oz are usually adequate for the sandy bottoms in this area. The rig itself has two attachment points for hooks, which just snap on the spreader rig.

As noted earlier, Sandfleas are an obvious and preferred natural bait for Pompano. They can either be caught live along our beaches or bought frozen from local tackle stores. Hooking a Sandflea is easy. Run the hook through the V-shaped flap on the flea's belly and rotate it on around so that the barb of the hook just protrudes from the top of the shell. Fresh dead shrimp, available at local fish markets, is a good second choice bait for Pompano. Big Pompano are occasionally caught on squid strips.

Jig fishing is rapidly become a popular second approach to catching Pompano. In this area, 3/8 to 5/8 oz white or beige colored jig heads with white, yellow, orange, hot pink, or pearl skirts have been the most successful. As was true with bait fishing, the jig should be worked through and along the troughs between the sand bars paralleling the beach. While you are doing that, keep your eyes open for schools of Mullet or Whiting. **Panhandle** area surf fishermen have found that Pompano, while not mingling, will follow along closely behind these schools.

On a concluding note, the following special miscellaneous tips might help your overall Pompano fishing success. First, if you are using jigs, sweeten the hook with a small Sandflea. Second, when trying to catch Sandfleas on the beach, watch for clusters of tiny V's in the sand as waves recede into the Gulf. The V's are caused by the antennas on the Sandflea's head and mark the spot where you should dig. Digging can be either with your hands, using half a minnow trap, or a Sandflea rake. Third, just for the heck of it, try a small chartreuse plastic crab rigged like you would a plastic worm in bass fishing. This has reportedly been a very hot number in recent months. Finally, don't cast out too far. To repeat and earlier point, Pompano will be in the troughs close to shore. Don't waste your time farther out!

Redfish

The Redfish, which is also called Red Drum or Channel Bass by many, is somewhat similar to the Black Drum in shape. The Redfish's coloration, however, is distinctly different. His body is a copperish iridescent color shading to copperish-red toward the back. As the fish matures, he becomes reddish-bronze all over. All Redfish have one or more black spots at the base of their tails. The Florida record for Reds is 51 pounds, 8 ounces.

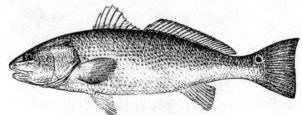

Thanks largely to the various restrictions imposed on catching Redfish, this fish has made an amazing comeback in this area. As the **Panhandle** fishing activity summary in Chapter 1 indicated, Redfish can now be caught year round in this area. Gratifyingly, divers routinely report large schools of Reds to 40+ lbs around area bridge pilings and along the jetties.

The Redfish is a bottom feeder who likes to eat a variety of things including shrimp, crabs, sandfleas, fingerling Mullet, Pinfish, Cigar Minnows and Alewife. One particularly effective way to catch Redfish has been with the latter two baits. Fishermen catch live Cigar Minnows and Alewife from around pier or bridge pilings using the rigs described earlier in this chapter. The live bait is immediately hooked on a fish finder rig with a 30-50 lb test mono leader, 3/0 hook and 2 oz to 4 oz egg sinker. Reds must be fished on the bottom. Sunup and/or an outgoing tide have seemed to provide the right conditions for aggressive feeding by resident Redfish. Reds will also hit a variety of lures. These include spoons (usually gold), deep diving plugs, metal squids, and plastic grubs and twister tails in many different sizes and colors. Particularly hot lures have included large Cordell Spots in blue and silver and black and silver, gold and firetiger Rat-L-Traps, and white nylon jigs with about a 4 inch piece of chartreuse plastic worm as a trailer. In the East end of the **Panhandle**, green and red and white jigs work very well too.

One relatively new (for this area) approach to catching Reds in some of their shallow water habitats is with floating/diving crankbaits. They are particularly effective where there is a hard, rough bottom in one to five feet of water that slopes off to a deeper open channel. While top water or subsurface plugs can be used in such spots, floater/divers are the only lures that can get down to the fish without getting hung up. Check your freshwater tackle box. You are looking for plugs that have relatively compact bodies, 2 ½ to 3 ½ inches long, and a big lip. When used, the plug should dive at a relatively steep angle, not get much deeper than five to six feet, and most importantly, achieve a wide, wobbling action on a slow retrieve. One productive lure recently has been the Mann's Crawdad in the quarter ounce size.

Legal size (18-27 inches) Redfish are great eating, with flesh that is ideally suited for blackening using commercially available Cajun seasonings. It is a taste treat you really must try.

Sailfish

The Atlantic Sailfish has one not surprising physical characteristic, an enormous dorsal fin. It is much higher than the greatest depth of its body and extends from its head to more than halfway down its body. The Sail's body is long and slender and dark steely blue on top and white on the bottom. His huge dorsal fin is bright cobalt blue and may be sprinkled with round black spots. The Sail's spear is long and the slender and often slightly curved. An Atlantic Sailfish has an average weight of around 40 pounds. The Florida record for Sailfish, however, is 116 pounds.

Each year, a small number of Sails are caught in ***Panhandle*** Inshore waters, usually by fishermen drifting live bait for something else. In addition to the various baitfish used for Kings and Blackfin Tuna, local Sailfish seem to be particularly fond of large live shrimp. Two areas where Sailfish catches have been reported are off Destin's Okaloosa Island Pier and Panama City's Dan Russell Municipal Pier.

Well rigged natural baits are often productive for Sails. Ballyhoo, Mullet, and Bonito strips are all used by local fishermen. Of these, Bonito strips frequently get the nod because their durability permits faster trolling speeds. If you are willing to go to the trouble of rigging Ballyhoo, it will usually pay off in fish. One popular terminal rig consists of a 5 or 6 foot length of 65-80 lb wire with a loop on one end and a good snap swivel at the other. The Ballyhoo is rigged to a 7/0 or 8/0 needle eye hook, with a 3/4 inch wire spike left on the wire wrap. This is used to pin the Ballyhoo's head. One end of a small rubber band is slipped over the spike, then streched around the head of the Ballyhoo and also hooked over the end of the spike. A 12 inch piece of wire with a loop on one end is attached to the eye of the hook with a haywire twist. The bait, and others pre-rigged like it, can then be very quickly attached to the snap swivel mentioned above.

Although a well-rigged natural bait is effective by itself, there are times when a skirt or Sea Witch lure can help. Traditionally effctive Sea Witch colors include blue and white, pink and blue, and red and black. A good rule of thumb is usually bright colors on bright days, darker colors combinations on darker days and early and late in the day.

Many fishermen looking for Sails try to pull as many lines as possible behind their boats. One or more of these lines are used for teasers. These can range from daisy chains of hookless small Mullet or plastic squid to single large hookless Ladyfish, Mullet, or horse Ballyhoo. Another choice is a large, thrashing mirrored plug. There are a number of lures that have also caught Sails locally. They include Moldcraft's Softhead Hookers and Birds, Tony Accetta Jelly Bellies, Arbogast's Reto's Rigs, and Boone's Airheads.

Sheepshead

The Sheepshead is a squatty shaped fish with pronounced black and silver stripes running vertically on its sides. It has strong, unnotched incisor teeth which are used to pick mollusks and crabs and scrape barnacles off rocks. The average weight of local area Sheepshead is 2-3 lbs, but fish to 10 lbs are not totally uncommon. Its fillets are pure white and delicious eating. The Florida record for sheepshead is 15 pounds, two ounces.

Sheephead are almost exclusively caught on bait. Althought once in a great while, one will take a small fly or jig, real food is the preferred approach. In the surf, fiddler crabs, sandfleas, hermit crabs, and fresh dead shrimp have all proven effective. Of these, fiddler crabs are superior.

Hooking fiddler crabs can be sporty. They do have claws which can give you a good pinch. To solve this problem, many fishermen use pliers to break off the big claw prior to baiting up. Putting a fiddler on your hook is easy. Hold him between your thumb and forefinger, right side up. Insert the hook point into the socket where the second leg from the back joins the body. Rotate the hook around, bring the hook point and barb out the back of the body shell. This method does not hurt the crab and he will remain alive and kicking.

The two hook spreader and fish finder rigs suggested for Pompano are also ideally suited for catching Sheepshead. You might want to use a smaller hook size (#1 or #2), however, depending on the size of bait. Whatever size hook you end up with, make sure it is substantial. Sheepshead can destroy flimsy wire hooks.

Frequently, when you least expect it, Sheepshead wander by. If you are unprepared (i.e. no live or dead shrimp, fiddler crabs, etc.) you are usually out of luck. However, if you just happen to have a soft plastic crab in your tackle box, try it. Rig it Texas style, with a slip sinker and quietly present it to the fish. They really will hit them, regardless of color.

Two other tips for catching your share of Sheephead may be helpful. First, if you are using live shrimp for bait, hook it through the tail rather than the head. Because a Sheepshead usually takes the head off the shrimp first, your hook in the tail will get him when he finishes off his meal. Second, to get the fish in the proper mood (hungry), take a piece of pipe, a hoe, or similar tool with you when you are fishing around pilings. Scrape the barnacles or oysters (both Sheepshead favorites) off the pilings for very effective natural chum.

Snapper

As was true with the Grouper family, there are a number of different kinds of Snapper present at various times in **Panhandle** area waters. For the sake of brevity, only four of the most common will be discussed here.

The Vermilion Snapper, known locally as the "Mingo", is the most common in area waters. Its entire body is reddish in color, with a series of short, irregular lines on its sides. Above the lateral line, it may have diagonal blue lines formed by spots on its scales. It may also have yellow streaks below the lateral line. Mingo is superb eating. An average fish will weigh about a pound and a half and catching a six pounder would be a real accomplishment.

The Snapper usually caught in the area's Bays and adjacent Inshore waters are typically called Black or Mangrove Snapper. It's correct name, however, is Grey Snapper. This fish's body is bronze-green on the top, shading in to brassy-red on its sides and light grey on its belly. It has a dark streak which runs from its nose across its eyes and then fades toward the dorsal fin. Some of the scales on the fish's sides have random darker markings. Although Grey Snappers have been caught to over 10 pounds, 1 or 2 lbs is considered a good fish. The Florida record is 16 pounds, eight ounces.

The Mutton Snapper is olive green on its back and upper sides with all its fins below the lateral line usually having a reddish tinge. The Mutton almost always has a bright blue line below each eye. Up to 15 pounds is a common weight, but the Florida record was a most impressive 27 pounds, six ounces.

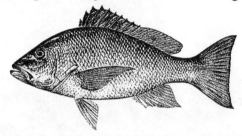

The Red Snapper is a medium sized fish that is relatively common up to 35 pounds and 30 inches in length. An averaged sized ***Panhandle*** area Red is considerably smaller. Not surprisingly, he is rosy-red on his upper body shading to lighter red on his lower sides and belly. His fins and eyes are also shades of red. The Red Snapper is usually found in schools which frequent an area with a hard bottom and adjacent structure of some sort. The world record Red Snapper weighted 46 pounds, eight ounces, and was caught in ***Panhandle*** area waters.

In Inshore and Offshore waters, a good rig for Red and other area Snapper is called, not surprisingly, a Snapper rig. Making one is easy. Using a 6 foot piece of 50 to 80 lb test mono, first make a loop at one end with a double surgeon's knot. Depending on the current, loop on an 8 to 16 oz. bank sinker. Next, make two droppers 16 and 32 inches above the sinker using the same surgeon's knot. Each dropper should be 10 to 16 inches long. Finally, tie on a barrel swivel 18 inches above the top dropper and attach hooks to the droppers by inserting the loops through the hook eyes and then doubling the loops back over the shanks of the hooks. Depending on the expected size of the resident fish, a 3/0 to 4/0 bronze hook is about right.

Two good dead baits for Red Snapper are whole Squid or Cigar Minnows. Fish these guys three to five cranks off the bottom to avoid ever present junk fish. A filleted Mingo is another deadly bait. Save the fillets for your dinner table--and use the Mingo carcass, hooked through the eye socket, to catch other, really big Red Snappers.

For larger Snapper, one other rig should be tried. It is the fish finder described in the earlier Amberjack section. Use live Pinfish, Alewife, Grunts, Croaker, etc. and try varying the depth of your bait in case the fish are suspending over the bottom structure.

For very large Snapper, a third rig might do the trick. Whole Cigar Minnows are the preferred bait. A fish finder rig is built by sliding an eight ounce egg sinkers on your line and then tieing the line to a black barrel swivel. Then tie a two and a half to three foot piece of a 80# test mono to the other side of the swivel. Finish off the rig with a 5/0 #085 Eagle Claw hook. To bait, pass the hook and about six inches of leader through the Cigar Minnow's eye socket. Then make a loop around the Minnow between its gills and the dorsal fin area. Insert your hook through the minnow's body just behind the anal vent. Slowly pull the leader back through the eye socket while aligning the hook's shank parallel to the minnow's body. The result should be the hook's point and barb exposed on one side and all slack in the leader around the body removed. You are now ready for a really big Snapper!

The Grey or Black Snapper is extremely difficult to catch. The bigger fish are very reluctant to hit anything that doesn't look entirely natural. Once hooked, they are also most adept at cutting lines on sharp edges anywhere in the area. A rig for this guy is simple. Tie a #6 or #8 bronze hook to the end of your line. Attach a split shot or rubber core sinker about 3 ft up your line. Use live shrimp (which you can buy) or small live Croakers or other small fish (which you must net) for bait. You must react immediately when a Snapper strikes or risk a cutoff. This fish is outstanding eating. Sometimes, feeding Black Snapper will just turn off. One way to get them going again is with a judicious application of cat food to the area. Be sure to use the canned stuff with a fish base. Another approach to Black Snapper fishing is off deep water docks at night. Tie a #1 or 1/0 bronze, short shank hook on the end of your line (#10 test mono). Use very small Bonito fillets for bait and no sinker. This combo really works well!

Spanish Mackerel

A Spanish Mackerel is dark bluish-brown on the top part of its body and silvery on its belly. It has golden spots above and below its lateral lines. It also has a dandy set of small razor like teeth. Spanish average 1 ½ to 3 lbs, but fish to 10 lbs are caught in ***Panhandle*** area waters. They are particularly good eating when cooked fresh on the grill . The Florida record for Spanish is 12 pounds.

As noted in the Species/Location Correlation Matrix in Chapter 1, Spanish can be caught in ***Panhandle*** area Bays, Surf, off Piers, and in Inshore waters. The following paragraphs highlight some points that may help you catch your share.

Much of the discussion on catching Bluefish on bait is directly applicable to also catching Spanish Mackerel.

Only two exceptions need to be mentioned. First, and although Spanish also have a formidable set of teeth, they are not quite as devastating as those worn by a Bluefish. Accordingly, terminal tackle can be lighter. Specifically, leader wire should be #1 or #2 and certainly not heavier than #3. In this regard, sometimes when the Spanish are being particularly difficult, local fishermen will switch to 30-50 lb test mono for leaders. As is true with Bluefish, black swivels must be used because Spanish are notorious for hitting brass ones. The other exception is the use of smaller baits. This is particularly true if you are using live bait or frozen cigar minnows.

Schoolie Spanish Mackerel will tear into almost any small lure when they move into an area. Nylon jigs, feather lures and spoons are traditionally effective. Regardless of what's used, Spanish can't seem to resist a darting action. You should use a rapid retrieve with regular snaps of your rod tip to make your lure jump and dart through the water.

Recently, three lures have had noteworthy success for Spanish in *Panhandle* area waters. The first is the old standby Gator spoon in 1/2 oz. and 3/4 oz. sizes. Make sure you use the version with the small fluorescent pink tab on the split ring. The second is the Gotcha in a variety of sizes and colors. The third is the almost unbelievable straw rig. This lure is nothing more than about 30 inches of heavy mono with a barrel swivel on one end and a 2/0 or so treble hook on the other. A two inch piece of McDonald's (yes, of the "Golden Arches") soda straw covers the shank of the treble hook. The rig is fished with a partially water-filled clear plastic casting bubble running free on your line above the barrel swivel. It is cast out as far as possible and then rapidly retrieved with frequent major popping actions with your rod tip. Fishing success with the straw rig has been truly extraordinary.

Another extraordinary lure, designed exclusively for trolling is worthy of mention. It's called a Mackerel Tree and has been deadly on Spanish Mackerel in the *Panhandle* area. The Mackerel Tree is nothing more than a heavy piece of mono with a barrel swivel on one end, four hooks sheathed in bits of brightly colored tubing spaced equidistant down the mono, and a snap swivel on the other end. Many fishermen attach a #1 or #2 Squid Spoon to the snap swivel. The rig is slow trolled where Spanish tend to hang out. Up to three or four nice fish at a time is not unusual.

Bait, too, can be used with some success for Spanish. Chunks of fresh or frozen mullet or cigar minnows fished with a short steel leader, 2/0 hook and no weight have done well on Spanish during late afternoon and evening hours.

Swordfish

Entire books have been written about catching this elusive denison of the deep. So, these comments will be concise. The color of a Swordfish's back varies between black, greyish blue, brown, metallic purple and bronze. It's underbelly is a dirty white. And, not too surprisingly, it has a long, flat sword-like upper jaw. Commercially caught Swordfish used to average 200 pounds but sadly, due to over-harvesting, average catch weights are now substantially less. The Florida record for a Swordfish is 612 pounds, 12 ounces. Swordfish steaks are a gourmet's delight.

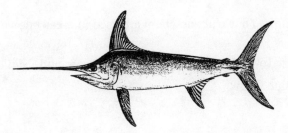

Trolling is always a popular method of catching Swordfish, although Desoto Canyon area fish are also taken by drift fishing at night with live bait. Squid, Bonito and small Tuna are all good baits. Fresh squid is much preferred over frozen, hook size must be at least 12/0, and monofilament leaders must test at least 200 pounds. Successful Swordfishermen in this area insure their bait's visibility at the required great depths by using battery powered lights and Cyalume glowsticks. The highest probability for Swordfish success is usually at night-- at depths between 600 and 1500 feet.

Tarpon

Tarpon are usually dark-blue to greenish-black dorsally, shading to bright silver on their sides and bellies. Fish from inland waters sometimes display brownish or brassy colors. ***Panhandle*** area Tarpon get big, with fish over six feet in length and 100 pounds not extraordinary. The Florida record for Tarpon is 243 pounds.

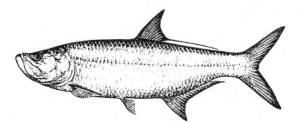

There are a number of ways to catch area Tarpon including artificial lures, flies, live bait and cut bait with chumming. Surface and subsurface lures seem to work equally well. Usual trolling plugs are jointed or lipped swimmers in a six inch length and weighing about an ounce and a half. Feathers and spoons, of course are comparably large. There are various ways of protecting the end of your line from chafing against the Tarpon's rough body. One effective approach is to use a short length (12-15 inches) of 100 pound test cable leader spliced through a leader sleeve to five feet of 40-50 pound test monofilament.

Fly fishing for Tarpon is considered a supreme angling thrill by many fishermen. A favorite fly for Tarpon is a yellow and orange splayed-wing streamer. All white or one with a touch of red, all yellow or red and yellow have also been proven choices over the years. The splayed wing tied with long 3-5 inch hackle feathers is ideal because it produces a fluttering action at the slightest rod movement. Area Tarpon have proven to be susceptible to a slow retrieve and the "breathing" of the wings that help animate the fly.

Another technique used in the ***Panhandle*** area involves chumming for Tarpon. The essence of this technique is simple. Fresh Mullet is used both for bait and as chum. Mullet strip baits are fished on the bottom using a terminal rig of five feet of 50 pound test mono and a short-shank, bronze-finish 3/0 hook. Other Mullet including carcasses are shredded up for chum. Your bait and chum are used in areas known to harbor Tarpon.

A variety of live baits can also be used effectively to catch Tarpon. These include Mullet, Cigar Minnows, large Alewife, Saltwater Catfish and Blue Crabs.

Triggerfish

The Gray or Common Triggerfish is a frequent inhabitant of both Inshore and Offshore bottom structure. It attains a respectable size of up to 10 lbs., with average weights of 1 to 2 lbs. It is usually gray in color with random darker markings and has an impressive set of dentures. The Triggerfish is difficult to clean because of its thick, heavy skin. However, the cleaning effort is well worth it, since the Triggerfish is delicious eating.

The two hook Snapper rig, described previously, is a good one to use for Triggerfish. Hook size should be reduced, however, to a #1 or #1/0 if Triggers will be the only anticipated catch. Relatively small pieces of frozen squid or fresh, dead shrimp are the best baits.

For what its worth, the Triggerfish gets that name because of the interaction of its three dorsal spines. The first spine is very large and bony and can be locked upright by the fish, or even by an angler after the fish has died. When locked, the big fin is immobile. That is a distinct advantage to the Trigger when something large is trying to swallow it. The fin can also be used as a wedge when a predator is attempting to pull the Trigger out of a hole. Other fish don't know the secret but anglers long ago learned that the second dorsal fin- the "trigger"- can be easily depressed to unlock the bigger one.

Tripletail

As is evident in the picture, the Tripletail is appropriately named. The combination of his upper and lower fins and his tail appear to give him three tails. Coloring varies widely, with black, brown and yellow predominant colors. The Tripletail attains a length up to three feet and can weigh over 30 pounds. It is a good eating and great fighting fish.

Tripletail are usually found around wrecks, buoys and floating or sunken debris. Live bait such as shrimp, clams and Mullet are preferred, but jigs and lures are successful at times. Small Pinfish will also tempt this guy on occasion.

96

Although Tripletail have been caught in Pensacola and Destin area waters, Apalachicola Bay is the premier spot for them. Called Sunfish by the locals, Tripletail average 15-18 pounds in the Bay in the June-July time frame. An all-tackle record of 32 pounds was set there several years ago and although it has since been broken, that fish remains the Florida state record.

One rig for live baiting shrimp includes the following: #2/0 hook; 18 inch, 30# test monofilament leader attached to a barrel swivel; a sliding one ounce egg sinker above the swivel; and a popping cork. The cork is just to help casting and for marking the bait. Don't pop it or you'll scare away Mr. Tripletail.

Trout

There are three kinds of Trout caught in the *Panhandle* area. The first is referred to locally as a White Trout although its correct name is Sand Sea Trout. This is a relatively small fish of 12-15 inches in length. Its body is pale silver in color without well defined spots. Its upper body has a yellowish tint to it. Because of its feeding habits and food preferences, it's a good fish for young folks to catch.

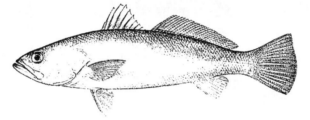

The second kind of Trout available in *Panhandle* waters is the Silver Sea Trout. The Silver is the smallest member of the Trout clan, usually weighing a half a pound or less. Its back is the color of pale straw, its sides are silvery, its belly white and it has no distinct pigmentation.

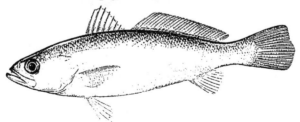

The final kind of Trout available to *Panhandle* fishermen is the Spotted Sea Trout, known affectionately as a "Spec". This fish has a relatively long, slender body which is dark grey above with sky blue reflections shading to a silvery color below. The upper part of its body including the dorsal and caudal fins is marked with numerous round, black spots. Mature Specs average about 4 lbs., with lunkers in this area sometimes going over 8 lbs. The Florida record for a Spec is 15 pounds, 6 ounces.

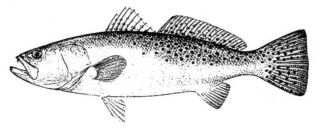

At any given time, all three kinds of trout will take either bait or lures. Preferred baits for Specs include live Shrimp, fingerling Mullet, small Croakers and Pinfish. Depending on the circumstances, the bait can either be fished by flylining or with an appropriately sized popping cork. One rig, particularly popular around Steinhatchee, works great with live shrimp. It uses a Float-Hi bobber with a fabric tie that allows your line free movement through the float to whatever depth you've chosen. Below the float, string on a 1/2 oz. slip sinker and then tie on a small barrel swivel. Three feet of 20-25# test mono and a hook appropriately sized for your live shrimp complete the rig.

The numbers and kinds of lures specifically designed to catch trout are almost mind-boggling. In this area, and at one time or another, all of the following have caught fish:

- Mirrolures- Floaters and sinkers in green and silver, black and silver, all silver, red and white, hot pink, iridescent orange and the new transparent and blue models. In the case of floaters, the models with propellers at both ends do very well in the warmer months.

- Rapalas and Rebels- Floaters, sinkers and small split backs in both silver and gold.

- Grubs and Twister Tails- Red, yellow and white heads all work at various times. Effective body colors include white, white with a firetail, chartreuse, chartreuse with a firetail, silver sparkle with a firetail, yellow, rootbeer and hot pink.

- Spoons- Small gold or silver.

- Plugs- Zara Spooks in red and white and mottled green and brown and Rat-L-Traps in silver, gold and fire tiger. One interesting variation on the Zara Spook should also be tried. Remove the rear hook from a Spook, and replace it with a 3 foot mono leader with a grub tied on the end. The slashing action of the plug seems to attract the Trout, which then hit the grub.

Of all the baits in the world for Specs, two are worthy of special mention. The first, Croakers, are absolutely superior whenever you can get them. When Trout are being very finicky about what they'll eat, they usually won't pass up a Croaker flylined or fished with a popping cork. The second bait, called Choafers locally (Pinfish), are also much enjoyed by Trout. Choafers are particularly effective in late Spring/early Summer when drifted across the many productive grass flats in the area. Unfortunately, neither Croakers nor Choafers are available at most bait shops. However, with a small cast net or minnow trap, you can usually get all the bait you want.

One caution is in order. Regardless of whether you are fishing bait or lures for Trout, don't horse a hooked fish. The Trout has a very soft mouth and any undue pressure will cause your hook to pull out. Be gentle but firm.

Wahoo

The Wahoo is a long, slender member of the Mackerel family. It has a long, tubular snout and a mouth full of very wicked teeth. Its body is dark green to steel blue on top, shading to paler silver on its sides. It also usually has narrow greyish yellow bars running vertically on its sides. Wahoo in this area average 15-25 lbs., but fish up to 100 lbs. are not unheard of. The Wahoo is a tremendous fighter and is reputed to be the fastest fish in the sea. They are delicious eating. Wahoo to 139 pounds have reportedly been caught on rod and reel.

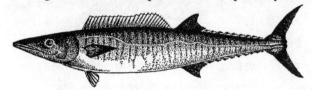

One of the hot tickets for Wahoo has consistently been large, trolling plugs pulled on down riggers. Offshore lipped favorites include Rapala's CD 18 Magnum Series, Bagley's DB-08 Diving Bang-O-B, Rebel's Jaw Breaker and the Mirrolure MR III. Three other unlipped plugs, the Boone Cairns Swimmer, Williamson Lures' Australian Runner and Braid's Flashdancer, also produce good fish. Bait-O-Matic is another family of lures that works very well for Wahoo, as well as for Dolphin, Marlin and Tuna. The Bait-O-Matic can be used effectively with dead or live bait or without dressing.

White Marlin

A White Marlin is the smallest member of the Marlin family, with an average weight of 50-60 lbs. and a maximum of 160 lbs. The upper part of his body is brilliant greenish blue, which changes abruptly to silvery white at about the lateral line. His belly is white. He has light blue or lavender vertical bars on his sides and a bright blue dorsal fin that is spotted with black or purple. White Marlin are common up to about eight feet in length. They are not good to eat. The Florida record for White marlin is 161 pounds.

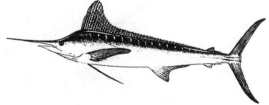

The White Marlin run in the Desoto Canyon area typically occurs in October and is eagerly awaited by **Panhandle** Offshore fishermen. There are usually lots of fish and they deserve their reputation of being the top Offshore light tackle quarry.

White Marlin will strike at almost any kind of lure, including spoons, feathers, whole fish and strip baits. Ballyhoo and Hoochie skirt combinations have proven particularly effective in this area. Sevenstrand and/or number 1220 Flying Fish Clones, fished six to nine waves back on an outrigger are a good complement to the skirted baits.

Whiting

The Whiting is a relatively small (10-16 inches) fish that is present in the area surf at least eight months of the year. It's basically silver in color with darker shaded areas running diagonally across its body. As a bottom feeder, its mouth is located under the point of its nose. While relatively small, the Whiting is delicious eating. A giant Whiting might weigh three pounds and a nice average fish about a pound.

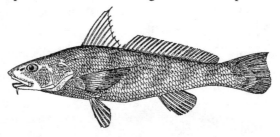

Whiting are most frequently caught on bait. While they are known to feed on a variety of crabs, shrimp and mollusks, small pieces of fresh dead shrimp are the preferred bait in this area. Both spreader and fish finder rigs work well with hook sizes ranging from one to six.

Another way to catch Whiting is with ultra light spinning tackle and tiny 1/8 oz. and 1/4 oz. jigs. Four or six lb. test line should be used with a 2 ft. piece of 20 lb. test leader attached on the end via a #12 barrel swivel. Nylon or feather jigs in yellow, white or green all seem to work well. As with Pompano, watch for and cast to these guys in the troughs that parallel the beach. Also, as with Pompano, add a small Sandflea to your jig to enhance your success.

Yellowfin Tuna

The Yellowfin is the most brilliantly colored of the Tunas, with a poorly defined golden yellow stripe on its upper sides and a much brighter yellow on its fins. Its lower sides commonly have white spots and vertical streaks. Yellowfins have a traditional Tuna shape and an average weight between 20 and 120 pounds. They're great eating.

You never know about Yellowfins in Offshore waters. Sometimes they show up and sometimes they don't. Migrating Yellowfins seem to randomly visit the area, remain for a few days to a week or two to feed, and then vanish.

When Yellowfin are around, daisy chains are an effective way to catch them. Specifically, a group of artificial plastic lures are rigged in series, with a large Tuna hook in the last lure in the chain. Lures strung like this range from standard Marlin lures to soft plastic imitation squids. One variation on this that also works well is to use a stainless steel spreader bar. In this approach, spreader bars are used to trail a pattern of 9 to 11 plastic squids with a hook only in the last lure.

The use of birds is another approach to try. A bird, sporting a wing of wood or plastic, is strung in line on the heavy mono leader ahead of the lure. This arrangement simulates a predatory fish chasing a smaller fish that flutters and splashes in front of it. A wide variety of lures can be used behind birds. Regardless of which one you choose, don't overlook the importance of color. The consensus in this area seems to be light and bright. Green, yellow, orange, light blue and hot pink are all popular colors.

Natural and Artificial Baits

In this section, we'll recap the baits that have proven effective in catching **Panhandle** area gamefish. We'll start by reviewing commonly used natural baits, both alive and dead. A summary of popular plastics will conclude the section.

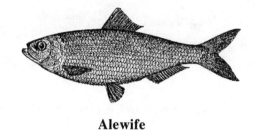

Alewife

- Catch them yourself by snagging, using an "Alewife Rig" (see King Mackerel section) or with a castnet
- Great for all area pelagic species (fish that spend their lives close to the surface as opposed to bottom dwellers)
- A particular favorite of big Kings and Specs in the Fall

Balao

- In this area, predominantly an Offshore bait for billfish
- Available frozen at many tackle stores
- Sometimes can be purchased pre-rigged

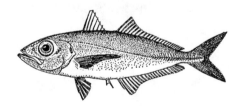

Bigeye Scad

- Excellent live bait for Offshore big game fish-- a White Marlin favorite
- Catch your own using "bait catcher rigs", small jigs or spoons
- Also known as Goggle-Eye Scad or Goggle-Eye Jack.

Blackfin Tuna

- One of the commonest items in the Blue Marlin's diet
- Catch your own using live bait or a variety of lures
- You can always eat your bait if a Marlin doesn't

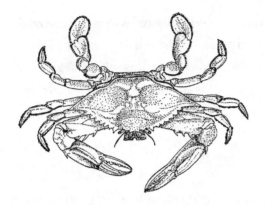

Blue Crab

- In varying sizes, a great bait for a variety of fish including Reds, Flounder, Sheepshead and Black Drum
- A particular favorite of the Cobia, who is also known as "Crab Cruncher"
- If you insert your hook where the second leg from the back meets the shell and rotate it on out the back of the shell, the crab will stay alive indefinitely
- You catch your own using a dip net or trap

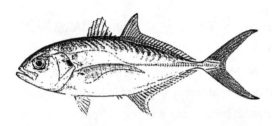

Blue Runner

- Commonly called a "Hard Tail"
- Edible in its own right
- You catch your own Inshore trolling, casting or still fishing with bait
- A superior live bait for slow trolling for King Mackerel and Blackfin Tuna

Bonito

- Easy and fun for you to catch your own using lures or bait
- An important part of a Swordfish's diet
- Superior bait for Shark due to its oily, bloody flesh
- A few tackle stores have frozen Bonito for Shark fishermen

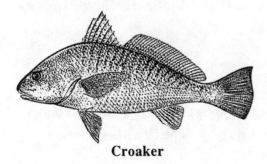

Croaker

- A superior and consistently effective live bait for Specs, Reds and Flounder
- You catch your own on the bottom using bits of dead shrimp or with a cast net
- Big Croakers are good to eat too

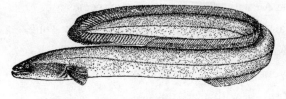

Eel

- The premier live bait for Cobia during their Spring migration along **Panhandle** beaches
- Some tackle shops stock them in season but they're expensive
- A sandy hand makes holding them while baiting up much easier
- It's almost impossible to catch an Eel in a live well. Therefore, put them in a cooler on a towel over ice. The ice will make them sluggish and easy to catch. They recover quick in water
- Always hook an eel through the head (mouth) if you want to control it. If hooked through the back, it will dive.

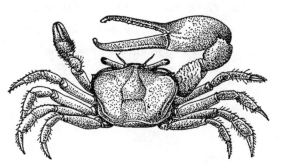

Fiddler Crab

- Bait of choice for Sheepshead, but equally good for Black Drum, Redfish, Flounder and Pompano
- Hook like a Blue Crab- hook in at second leg joint and rotate barb out the back
- Many tackle shops carry live Fiddlers- but you can often catch your own in rotting wood or in rocks/grass along the water line

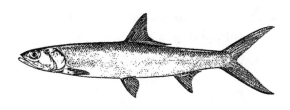

Ladyfish

- Sometimes called "Skipjack" and known as "poor man's Tarpon"
- Catch your own along the beach using small jigs, spoons and plugs
- Twelve to 24 inch Ladyfish, rigged with an egg sinker under the chin and an 8/0 hook through the lower jaw effective for Blue marlin
- A Tarpon won't refuse a live Ladyfish

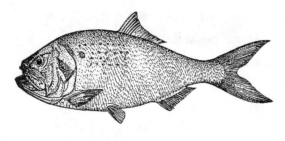

Menhaden

- Like the Alewife, good for all pelagic species
- A "major food group" for Bluefish, Swordfish, Tuna, Reds, Kings, et al.
- Catch your own with "bait catcher", "gold hook", or similar rigs or with a cast net
- Oily flesh makes chum made out of these guys particularly effective

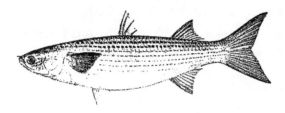

Mullet

- One of the most versatile and effective natural baits
- In its live form, what it catches is only a function of size- ie. a two inch "fingerling" will catch you a one pound Flounder while a two foot long Mullet will entice a 50+ pound "smoker" King
- Mullet strip baits, particularly when used with a variety of skirts, are great for many Inshore and Offshore species
- Mullet chunk baits are a continuing Tarpon favorite
- You catch your own Mullet with a cast net

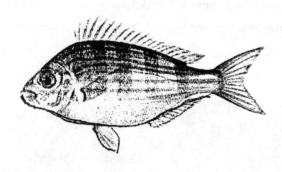

Pinfish

- Also known as a "Choafer"
- Another of the most versatile and effective live baits
- A favorite of Specs, Reds, Flounder, Cobia, Snapper, Grouper, Blackfin Tuna et al.
- Can be bought at a few tackle stores or marinas. Otherwise you catch them in a minnow trap or with a small hook and bits of shrimp or cut bait
- Fun for the kids to catch with their Zebcos

Sandflea

- Also known as a Sandbug, Molecrab or Sandcrab
- Some bait shops have them frozen. You catch them on the beach along the surfline
- Superior for Pompano and good for Reds, Sheepshead, Black Drum and sometimes Flounder
- Can be frozen successfully if you "blanche" them in boiling water for five seconds first

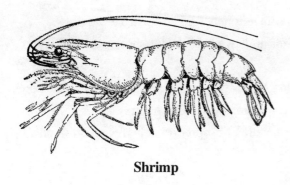

Shrimp

- Probably the single most commonly used natural bait in the **Panhandle** area
- Most bait shops have live shrimp year round
- Most popular place to hook a live shrimp is just behind where the pointy carapace or horn joins the head. Don't put your hook in the black spot just behind that (his brain) because that will kill him
- Trout, Reds, Sheepshead, Black Drum, Pompano, Flounder, Black Snapper and many others will fight for live shrimp. Most of the same fish will hit fresh dead shrimp as a second choice
- For what its worth, when you are using live shrimp in the wintertime, don't be surprised to see them lying on their sides in your bait bucket. That's a normal reaction to cold. They'll straighten up when you put them on a hook
- "The bait" for Flounder

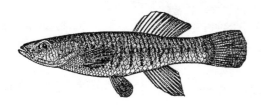

Striped Killifish

- Routinely called "Bull Minnow" in the **Panhandle** area
- Most bait shops carry live Bulls most of the year
- Specs, Reds and Black Snappers will take Bull Minnows now and then
- The biggest Bulls are sometimes effective for Grouper in area bays

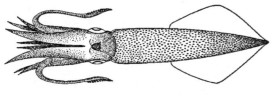

Squid

- Fresh or frozen, squid trolled whole are good for Tunas, Marlin, Swordfish etc.
- Cut squid, either in chunks, strips or whatever, consistently works for Flounder, Pompano, Whiting, Black Sea bass, Triggerfish and a variety of other area fish
- At certain times of the year, you can catch your own squid in **Panhandle** waters. Usually however, it is a purchase item

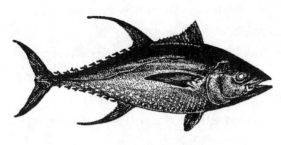

Yellowfin Tuna

- Blue Marlin routinely feed on small Yellowfins
- Watch for birds while in the Offshore Desoto Canyon area
- If feeding Yellowfins are attracting the birds, catch one or more with small live baits or lures
- Put a live Yellowfin, appropriately rigged, down on a downrigger
- Strap in!
- As noted earlier, you can always eat your bait if a Blue doesn't!

So much for natural baits. We'll now close out this section with an admittedly cursory overview of artificials that have been proven performers in the *Panhandle* area. As in other parts of Florida and the world, for that matter, imagination and experimentation are the keys to success in selection of lures. The guys who consistently catch the most and biggest fish on artificials-- are usually the guys who aggressively pursue new and better ways to convince their target that it really does want to eat a piece of plastic, lead or mylar.

Specific colors for each lure noted in figure3.0 were deliberately omitted. The "best" color for any given lure on any given day is very much a function of where you're fishing. Colors that work well in the Pensacola area, for example, might not work at all in the Panama City area. The best approach is to check with a local tackle store or marina for the hot "color tip" of the day.

— PERSONAL NOTES —

Panhandle Gamefish	Proven Artificials
Amberjack	Large grubs, twister tails, jigs, large jointed plugs.
Black Drum	#2 Clark spoons and jigs (occasionally).
Black Sea Bass	Small grubs, twister tails or jigs of any color, silver spoons.
Blackfin Tuna	Clark spoon, Soft head, Califorinia and No Alibi feathers, any plug resembling a Ballyhoo, Creek Chub Pikie, rubber squid skirts.
Bluefish	Tony Accetta Pet Spoons, Ragmop, tube lures, surface and diving plugs, jigs.
Blue Marlin	Softhead, C&H, Snider(large), Reto's Rigs, Boone's Airheads, R&S Small Teardrops, rubber squids, #1400 Sevenstrand Konahead, Kona Clone.
Bonito	Almost anything you've got. Chorme jigs with squid skirts are deadly.
Cobia	1 1/2-3 oz. jigs, plastic eel, tube lure, large swimming plugs, 65M Mirrolure, Cordell Spots.
Dolphin	Baby Dusters, small feathers, Moldcraft hookers, Dolphin Jr's & Sr's, Jelly Bellies, a variety of Marlin lures with 9/0-12/0 hooks, Boone Sea Minnows.
Flounder	Small jigs, twister tails and grubs, 3/8-1/2 oz. gold spoons, small deep running plugs that root in the bottom.
Grouper	Large deep diving lipped plugs, large grubs and twister tails, Yo hoho and Sea Strike metal jigs in Mackerel colors, Tony Accetta spoons, Capt Action and Squid silver 6" spoons, 103 and 113 series Mirrolures, 116 AXSI Bombers, and 1oz Rat-L-Traps.
Jack Cravalle	Topwater "chugger" plug, Bucktail jigs, spoons, 85M Mirrolures, Zara Spooks.
King Mackerel	Dusters, Tony Accetta Pet spoons, Crippled Alewife spoon, Cordell Spots, 113 series Mirrolures, Cisco Kid, Rapala CC-18, Depth Raiders, jigs.
Pompano	3/8-5/8 oz. jigs, plastic grub and shad tails.
Redfish	Johnson spoons, jigs, crank baits, surface chuggers, grubs, twister tails, Tony Accetta Hobo Spoon, Hot Flashes, Sea Dudes.
Sailfish	Moldcraft Softhead Hookers and Birds, Tony Accetta Jellie Bellies, Arbogast's Reto's rigs, Boone Airheads, rubber squids.
Sheepshead	Small flies and jigs (once in a great while).
Snapper	2-5 oz. jigs tipped with 9-12 inch white, glow in the dark plastic worm, (for Blacks-7M Mirrolure, small floating Rapalas and Rebels).
Spanish Mackerel	Mackerel Tree, Straw Rig, small spoons, Rat-L-Traps, top water Bang-O-Lure jigs, gator spoons.
Swordfish	Unknown.
Tarpon	Jigs, grubs, 52M Mirrolure, Rattlin Flash, Bagley's Finger Mullet, 72M Mirrolures, Storm's Threadfin Minnow.
Triggerfish	Jigs tipped with squid or shrimp (occasionally).
Tripletail	Plastic and Bucktail jigs in several colors.
Trout	Jigs, many Mirrolure models including 52M26, 25MRG, and 33 MR2-4, plastic twister tails, Smithwick's Devil Horse, Cordell Crazy Shad, Cotee gold spoons.
Wahoo	Deep trolled Terminator, black and red No Alibi with a Ballyhoo, Magnum Rapala, Mann's Stretch 25+, Rebel Jawbreaker, Bagley DBO10.
White Marlin	Hoochie skirt and Ballyhoo, Sevenstrand or No.1220 Flying Fish Clone, Rito's Rigs, Boone Airhead, R&S Small Teardrops.
Whiting	Jigs.
Yellowfin Tuna	Spreader rigs with 9-11 plastic squids or "birds" ahead of bright colored skirted plastics, Magnum Rapalas, feathered jigs.

Figure 3.0 - **Proven *Panhandle* Area Artificials**

TACKLE REQUIREMENTS

The tackle used effectively in the waters along the *Panhandle* is as diverse as the kinds of fish that can be caught, Some suggestions are presented below for each of the major types of fishing available in the *Panhandle* area.

For most species in the Surf, light freshwater-type tackle works just fine. Rods from five to seven feet in length and either spinning, closed face, or bait casting reels are more than adequate for fishing the troughs. Six to ten pound test line is about right for Pompano, Flounder, Sheepshead, and Whiting. The same kind of tackle works great for area Bays.

Slightly heavier tackle may be in order if you intend to pursue Bluefish, Redfish, Spanish and Northern Mackerel, or Sharks. For these, rods to nine or more feet, open faced spinning reels, and eight to fifteen pound test line are about right. This kind of outfit will permit the longer casts necessary while having the extra power to effectively fight these larger fish.

Regardless of the kind of fish you're after, a sand spike is almost a necessity in surf fishing. Most are nothing more than a piece of large diameter plastic pipe with a point on one end. They're cheap to buy or make and infinitely useful to hold your rod and reel while you're baiting up, changing lures, or waiting for a bite.

For Piers and area jetties and depending on the kinds of fish you're after, two different kinds of tackle are required. If you intend to fish in the surf close to the beach (Pompano, Whiting, Flounder, etc.), think light. Bait casting and fresh water spinning gear with six to ten pound test line is ideal. If you intend to fish farther out (King Mackerel, Cobia, etc.), heavier equipment is in order. A medium action, seven to nine foot spinning rod and a large dependable spinning reel loaded with at least three to four hundred yards of fresh fifteen to twenty five pound test line are essential. Several tackle stores, bait shops and piers in the area have this kind of tackle available at reasonable rental rates.

Light tackle with eight to twelve pound test line is about right for catching Trout, Flounder, Snapper, Sheepshead, etc., in the area's bays, bayous and sounds. Ultra light tackle with four to six pound test line is also a lot of fun for catching these guys. If you intend to go for bigger game (Tarpon, Cobia, Kings, Jack Cravalle, etc.), you'll want to use much stouter equipment. For these guys, two different setups are required. To successfully land a Jack, for example, you'll want to use six to seven foot, medium action spinning rod matched with an open faced spinning reel sufficiently large to hold two hundred to three hundred yards of twenty to forty pound test line. Your reel must have a smooth, fully functional drag. For the giant Black Drum that inhabit the area, an Inshore bottom fishing setup is about right. A five to six foot medium action rod paired with a well maintained 4/0 reel with at least two hundred yards of thirty pound test line will give both you and the fish a chance.

If you're going to try all the kinds of fishing available Inshore and you want to maximize your sport in the process, you will need up to four rod and reel combinations. These are summarized below:

- King Mackerel, Bonito, Blackfin Tuna, and perhaps a stray Wahoo- Effective trolling for these fish requires a five to six and a half foot glass, fiberglass or graphite boat rod. It should have a medium or heavy action since you may be pulling planers or large diving plugs from time to time. Roller rod guides are a good feature, but not critical to success. The rod should be rated for somewhere between twenty and fifty pound test line. Your reel should be a well lubricated 6/0 loaded with at least two hundred fifty to three hundred yards of fresh, quality, line. The reel's drag must be fully functional and absolutely smooth during operation. For this kind of trolling, successful fishermen usually set their strike drag tension at approximately one-quarter of the rated strength of their line.

- Inshore bottom fishing- A five to six foot, medium action rod, rated for fifteen to thirty pound test line is about right for this kind of fishing. It should be paired with a well maintained 4/0 reel with at least a two hundred yard line capacity. As an aside, many successful bottom fishermen in the area prefer medium weight spinning tackle for this kind of fishing. That's because this kind of tackle is usually lots lighter and has a much more rapid retrieve.

- Casting for Cobia- Distance and precision are the name of this game. Accordingly, a six to seven foot medium action (1-3 oz lures) spinning rod works well. It should be matched with an open faced spinning reel sufficiently large to hold two hundred to three hundred yards of twenty to forty pound test line. Use of line in the lower end of this range absolutely requires a smooth, fully functional drag.

- Casting for Dolphin- As noted above, at various times, tide lines, weed lines, etc., form Inshore. Schoolie Dolphin take up residence and the fun begins. Break out your light spinning gear, with six to twelve pound test line and have the thrill of a lifetime.

Although tackle requirements for Offshore trolling are almost open ended, they don't have to be. Unless you're independently wealthy, requirements can be constrained by focusing on the area you plan to fish. Many local area fishermen, for example, specialize in mid-range trolling from thirty to sixty fathoms out. Lighter tackle can be used in this area, with thirty pound class gear quite adequate for all but the biggest fish. Targets of interest would include Dolphin, Wahoo, White Marlin, Sailfish, and Blackfin Tuna. For bottom fishing, your tackle should be relatively heavy. A popular combination includes a seven to seven and a half foot solid glass rod, a 6/0 reel loaded with one hundred pound test line (either mono or Dacron), a one hundred twenty five pound test leader, and a 5/0 or 6/0 hook. Because up to twenty oz sinkers are often required, some fishermen use electric motors on their reels. And then, there's Blue Marlin tackle.....for a mere $1500 or so, you, too can own a nice seven foot Murry Brothers "Master" series big game trolling rod and a Penn International 130 ST two speed reel. The price does not include the cost of 950 yards of 130# test line required to fill the reel. Oh well....

CHAPTER 4

SPECIAL SUBJECTS

Introduction

There are three questions frequently asked by both visitors to and residents of the *Panhandle* area-- that sometimes don't get answered very well. The questions are:

- "Where can I take my kids to catch some kind of a little fish?"
- "How do you catch Blue Crabs around here?"
- "Can you fly-fish for anything in this area?"
- "Are there any scallops left in Florida?"

Hopefully, this chapter will provide helpful answers to all questions.

Fishing For The Younger Set

There are a number of places to take kids to catch small fish. Some are obvious; others may not be. First, if you live near or are staying anywhere on the water-- bay, harbor, beach, etc.--they can fish right there. The rig and bait for all these areas are the same. Any kind of freshwater spinning or bait casting rod and reel will work just fine. So will the plastic Mickey Mouse rod and reel combos from Kmart. Tie a #6 or #8 bait holder hook directly to the end of the line. Then squeeze on a split shot weight about eight inches up the line. It should only be heavy enough to allow casting. Now, make a run down to the local fish market and buy a quarter pound of their cheapest fresh dead shrimp. Peel the shrimp and cut it into pieces just big enough to cover the hook. You are ready to catch small fish.

If you're not staying on the water, there are many other convenient places you can drive to for angling action. All of the city, county, state, and federal parks identified in chapter two are great spots for young people to fish. And, as an aside, Dad, make sure you have a light rod and reel readily available while you're helping the kids. More often than not, what they catch will be great bait for you to hook on under a popping cork for any Trout or Redfish that may be in the area. Or, put the kid's catch on the bottom with a slip rig for Flounder that may be close by.

Regardless of where you and the kids end up, your catch will probably include some or all of the following: Croaker, Pinfish, Grunt, Saltwater Catfish, and Puffer Fish. The first three are good eating and, as noted a moment ago, make great live bait for larger species. The latter two are not edible and should be handled with care due to their nasty spines.

Crabbing For The Entire Family

Crabbing is a favorite pastime in the *Panhandle* area. The Blue Crabs grow large, are delicious eating, and are relatively easy to catch. There are a number of important things to know about catching crabs and crabbing in this area. This discussion will hopefully cover them all. First, we'll talk about the crabs themselves- where they come from, how they live, and what becomes of them. After this short biology lesson, we'll cover where and how to catch them and any laws that may apply. A short lesson on cooking and cleaning is also included.

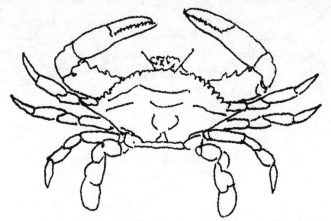

Figure 4.0 - **Blue Crab - Top View**

Blue Crabs in the area bays, sounds, etc. are a dull, olive green in color with some blue usually on the claws. Sometimes they have barnacles and other minute plant life growing on their top shells. Blue Crabs living in the surf, however, are usually a beautiful, bright blue. Regardless of where they reside, all Blue Crabs have a white or cream colored underside. The Blue Crab belongs to the family of swimming crabs because its last pair of legs are flattened into paddles for swimming.

Male Blue Crabs are easy to identify. Their abdominal aprons are in the shape of an inverted "T". Females are even easier to spot. First, they all have bright red/orange tips on their claws ("painted fingernails"). Males do not. Second, a sexually mature female has a semi-circular bell-shaped abdominal apron as contrasted with the male's inverted "T". Figure 4.1 provides sketches of Mr. and Mrs. Blue Crab.

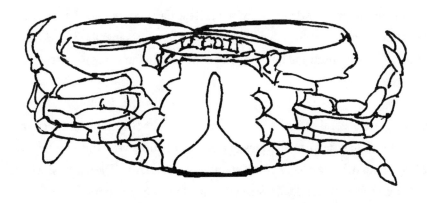

Male

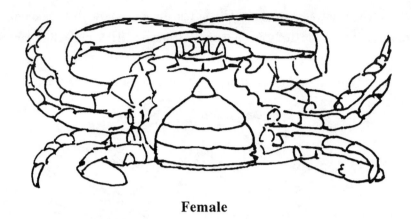

Female

Figure 4.1 - **Blue Crabs - Bottom View**

Blue Crabs grow by periodically shedding or "molting" their old bony exterior skeletons. They do this because these exo-skeletons are made of a substance which has no growth cells in it. Females molt 18-20 times over the course of their lifetimes; males some 21-23 times. In the period immediately following a molt, both sexes are totally soft, vulnerable and to some crab connoisseurs, the epitome of great eating. Left in the water, newly molted crabs harden rapidly. New shells become stiff in about 12 hours, crinkly hard in 24 hours and fully hardened in 72 hours. A Blue Crab's life expectancy is approximately three years, with males tending to outlive females. A big Blue Crab in this area is about eight inches wide from point to point across the top of the shell. The average size is somewhat less.

Blue Crabs are year round residents of all local waters. As will be noted in a moment, as water temperatures climb in the Summer, they can be found in increasingly shallow water. But as water temperatures dip into the fifties late in the year, they head in the other direction for the deepest water around. Once there, they bury themselves in the bottom. Their metabolism slows and they enter a period of dormancy. Only the warmth of an impending Spring can bring them out again. So much for the biology and physiology of a Blue Crab.

Springtime brings out the crabs everywhere. They're in all the bays, sounds and bayous. They're in deep water and shallow water alike. And, as water temperatures rise, the crab's metabolism does too. As a result, far less time is spent buried in the bottom and far more time is devoted to an aggressive search for food. In essence, they become easy prey!

In June and July, there are several effective ways to catch lots of Blue Crabs. Since the crabs are thickest in water that's at least four feet deep, techniques that are compatible with this depth work best. Traditional, rectangular wire traps baited with fish carcasses are always effective. These traps, which can be purchased for around $15, can be tossed out off docks, sea walls and the like or dropped off of a boat using some kind of a float to mark the spot.

Another successful technique involves the use of different kind of traditional crab trap. These traps, made out
112

of heavy cord or wire, are available at most tackle stores for less than $5. Their use is simple. A piece of some kind of bait is tied to the bottom of the trap. Personally, we have always had the best luck with and always use cut pieces of fish. It is then lowered to the bottom where, in the case of a wire trap, its sides collapse horizontally outward; or with a cord trap, it just lies flat. Unless the water is very clear and you can see the crab come in to eat, just pull either of these traps in (briskly) every few minutes to check for occupants. These traditional traps work well off any dock, such as the many nice ones at all area waterfront parks. Don't forget a covered basket or bucket in which to keep your catch alive.

Another more challenging approach requires at least two people, one or more baited lines, and a long handled crab dip net. Rigging for this technique is simple. Tie a reasonable sized hook (1/0) on the end of a 20-30 ft piece of fishing line. Then tie on any kind of weight about 12 inches above the hook. Finally, cut up any small fish you or the kids may have caught and put a chunk on the hook. Throw the bait out, let it sink to the bottom, and then hold the line very lightly in your hand. You'll feel a crab grab the bait and start eating. When this happens, start pulling in the line slowly but steadily. More often than not, the crab won't let go of his meal. When he gets in range of your crabbing partner's dip net, quietly get the net under him and lift up rapidly. This kind of crabbing is particularly suited to old docks with adjacent deep water, where the really big crabs hang out!

In August, September and sometimes early October, another kind of crabbing comes to the forefront. During this period, local crabs get really shallow- all around the area bays, sounds and bayous. Then the fun begins. The best way to catch these guys is just to wade the shallows with a dip net and scoop away. But, you have to be faster than they are! When you see them "dive" into the bottom, you can scoop into the sand from behind to catch them. It's literally that easy. Also, grassy areas on an outgoing tide are usually very productive too.

Another fun variation of this approach becomes possible in the same time frame. During these months, Blue Crabs that live in the Gulf come into the surf to spawn. Although they're there during the day, they are very difficult to see. But, at night, it's an entirely different story. The knee deep water along all our beaches becomes alive with frolicking crabs. A flashlight and a dip net are all you need to catch a bucket full. But, just remember, all those crabs you catch are going to have to be cooked and cleaned. Don't keep more than you can handle in this department.

An important note of caution on wading for crabs is appropriate. Regardless of where you wade, scuff your feet as you move along. There are Sting Rays in all our waters and they can cause a painful wound if you happen to step on one. Fortunately, they are very timid creatures and will move out of your way as soon as they hear you coming.

Before we stop talking about catching and start talking cooking and cleaning, a couple of words on the law are probably appropriate. Specifically, Florida salt water fishing regulations DO apply to crabbing. Translated, this means all kids under sixteen are unaffected; state residents need a saltwater fishing license if they're crabbing out of a boat; and out-of-state folks need a license regardless of where and how they crab. There is no minimum size limit on Blue Crabs but the bag limit is 10 gallons per day per person. You also cannot keep female crabs carrying eggs, which are orangish brown and usually all around the "apron" part of her shell.

Cooking your crabs is very easy. Make sure they are still alive. You just don't want to take a chance on cooking any crab that's dead. Given you've got a good lively crowd, standby to make steam. Depending on how many you've got, use an appropriately large pot with a lid. In the pot, use either a wire basket that's been designed for the purpose, or some kind of rack to keep the crabs up off the bottom. Add about an inch or so of water (with or without seasoning) and bring it to a boil. Dump in the crabs when the water is boiling, quickly put on the lid (the crabs will be anxious to avoid the free sauna!), and let the steam do the rest. Twenty minutes later, your crabs will be perfectly cooked and bright red in color.

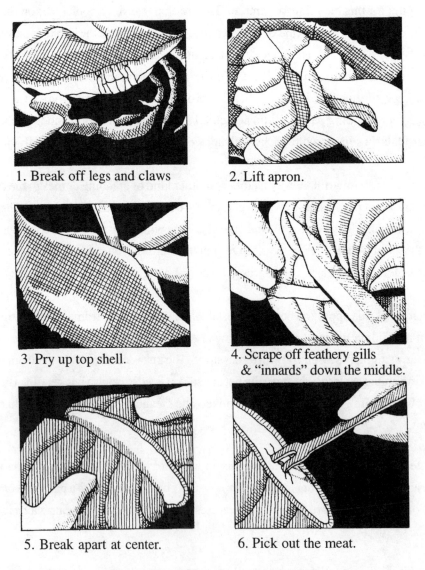

1. Break off legs and claws   2. Lift apron.

3. Pry up top shell.   4. Scrape off feathery gills & "innards" down the middle.

5. Break apart at center.   6. Pick out the meat.

Figure 4.2 - **"Cleaning your Crabs"**

Cleaning Blue Crabs isn't difficult, but it does get tedious if you have a lot. First, break off all the legs and claws where they join the body. Throw the legs away and save the claws for a feast. Next pry up the abdominal apron we talked about earlier. Put your thumb where the apron attaches to the upper shell. Pull the top shell off the crab's body. Then, using a dinner knife, scrape out/off the crab's innards down the center of the body and the gills on either side. Now, using thumb and forefinger, break off the eye and mouth section on the front. After a thorough rinsing, you're ready to get serious. Break the crab in half at the center. You now have two pieces of body that each has many small compartments full of pure meat. Your final challenge--get that meat out without any bits of shell or cartilage sneaking into your crabmeat. Now you know why crabmeat is so expensive to buy!

After all the fun and hard work of catching, cooking, and cleaning is over, it's time to reap the reward. It's eating time. Not surprisingly, with a delicacy like crab, there are lots of world class ways to prepare your catch. My wife has graciously agreed to share some of our family favorites with you. She calls herself a "dump cook", dumping in a little of this and that, so her recipes frequently do not include precise measurements.

Blue Crab Cakes with Mustard Sauce

2-3 cups crabmeat

1 pack Ritz crackers (about 35) finely crushed

2 eggs, beaten

About 1/4 cup Hellmanns Mayonnaise +-

Generous splash Worcestershire sauce

Several splashes Tabasco sauce

1 tsp dry mustard

Salt & white pepper to taste

Peanut oil to cook in (2-3 Tbsp.)

In a bowl, mix crackers, eggs, mayo, Worcestershire, Tabasco, mustard and seasonings. As you add crabmeat, feel for cartilage you may have missed the first time around and remove it. Mix gently but thoroughly. Add mayo if mixture is too dry. This part may be made ahead and stored in the refrigerator until ready to cook and serve. Unfortunately, this is one of those dishes that doesn't do well if made ahead, and must be cooked and served on the spot for best results. Shape into patties about 3" in diameter and cook in a skillet in a small amount of peanut oil. This recipe usually makes enough to serve four. The real secret to it's incredible good flavor--the mustard sauce that goes on top: to about 1/4 cup sour cream, mix in 1 tsp. Poupon mustard. The sauce is a wonderful complement to the crab cakes!

Florida Blue Crab Soup

Makes 8-10 servings (about 1 cup each), and is a wonderful, rich winter treat using frozen crab

2 medium potatoes

2-3 cups crabmeat, fresh or frozen

1 medium onion

1/4 cup water

1 Tbsp. butter (stir in with onion)

1 Tbsp. butter (for white sauce)

1 Tbsp. flour

1 cup milk

Salt & white pepper to taste

Tabasco to taste (6-8 splashes)

Worcestershire to taste (try 1-2 Tbsp)

1 Tbsp. lemon juice

2 cups half & half (or mocha mix)

2 cups milk (1% or skim is fine)

1/4 cup plus 2 Tbsp. butter

About 1 tsp. grated lemon peel

Peel potatoes and cut into pieces. Cook in lightly salted water about 20 min. until tender. Mash potatoes until smooth. Set aside. Go through crabmeat again for missed shell/cartilage. Set aside.

Cut onion into large pieces. Puree with water in blender or food processor. Melt 1 Tbsp. butter in skillet; stir in onion and cook for 5 minutes, stirring constantly. Set aside.

Make a white sauce with butter, flour and 1 cup of milk and seasonings. This can be done in a microwave or in a saucepan on the stove.

Mix in lemon juice gradually, stirring constantly to prevent curdling. Stir in potatoes, half & half and 2 cups of milk. Add crabmeat, 1/4 cup plus 2 Tbsp. butter, and grated lemon peel. Simmer uncovered over low heat about 10 minutes and it's ready to serve.

Nice to garnish with thin slice of lemon floater sprinkled with paprika for color.

Cinco Bayou Crab Casserole

3 Tbsp butter or margarine

3 Tbsp flour

Salt & white pepper to taste

About 1/4 tsp dry mustard

1-1/2 cups milk

Worcestershire sauce to taste

Hot sauce to taste

1/4 cup Parmesan cheese

2-3 cups crabmeat, picked through for missed shell and cartilage

1 large can artichoke hearts, drained and trimmed and chopped into chunks

Ritz cracker crumbs mixed with Parmesan cheese

Prepare a white sauce by melting butter, stirring in flour, gradually adding milk and seasonings, cooking until thickened. Stirring constantly. (Or do it quick and easy in the microwave where you don't have to stir but twice!) Add Parmesan cheese and crabmeat. In a baking dish, arrange artichoke hearts in bottom. Pour crab mixture over artichoke chunks. Top with crumb/cheese mixture. Bake at 350 degrees for 30 min. or so. Four generous main dish servings. Six to eight appetizer servings. Elegant!

Well, that's the Blue Crab story in ***Panhandle*** waters. As noted at the outset, there are lots of crabs in all area waters and they're ready to be caught. For great good fun for the entire family- and delicious eating- give crabbing a try!

Fly-Fishing

Each year, a growing number of fishermen successfully attack ***Panhandle*** area waters armed only with their fly-rods. They catch fish and have a ball doing it. Fly-fishing in this area is here to stay. For 95 percent of saltwater fly-fishing, a 9' to 9'3" fly-rod, engineered to handle a nine-weight fly line is about right. A single action fly-reel with adequate capacity for fly-line and backing, and a smooth drag, makes a balanced combination. A standard, weight forward fly-line should be used to finish off the outfit.

Basic leader construction should include a butt section of 20-40 lb test mono, a class tippet and a short shock tippet. The butt section should be about two-thirds the length of the leader with the shock and class tippets 12 and 15 inches in length respectively. Overall leader length should be about nine feet. For fish with sharp teeth (i.e. Bluefish, Spanish Mackerel etc.), ignore what was just said about leaders. For these fish, wire is required. About four inches of 25-35 lb. test solid brown wire, attached to no more than two feet of tippet material is an effective rig.

There are a number of different fish that would be delighted to hit your fly in this area. Several of the most notable are highlighted below.

- Redfish in the shallows, for example, will hit a popping bug, and they're a pushover for a big feather-type streamer fly tied on a 1/0 or 3/0 hook. Bright colors help the fish see your fly. Accordingly, streamers tied with red hackle and yellow wings are good, as are the red hackle with orange wings. Redfish like a fast retrieve.

- Jack Cravalle also like a fast retrieve. A good fly has consistently been the Glass Minnow tied on a 1/0 or 3/0 hook.

- Spotted Sea trout, on the other hand, like the fly slow at first. Then, when the retrieve is speeded up, they dash for it and hit at the last moment. Specs seem to prefer red and yellow and red and white combinations in streamer flies, bucktails and popping bugs. Remember not to horse a trout because of its very soft mouth.

- Bluefish and Spanish Mackerel will also take flies and are not particular about color. White, yellow and a variety of combinations will all work. Remember, however, that these guys must be fished with the short piece of wire leader mentioned previously.

- For Whiting, small weighted flies in red and white or black and white patterns seem to draw the best results. Sinking fly-lines are helpful in aiding a fly to creep along the bottom.

- Sheepshead are one of the toughest fish to fool with a fly-- some say even tougher than a Permit. A Sheepshead's small mouth means you'll have your best shot with small flies. In this regard, tiny Bonefish flies often work well, with black or brown being good colors. And, if you're not a fanatical purist, sweeten your fly with a tiny bit of fresh shrimp. You'll increase your success ratio by a factor of 10. Some other bottom-bumper flies you might consider include the Crazy Charlie, Aztec Pink Shrimp, Arbona's Shrimp and the Blue Tail Fly.

Fly-fishing for King Mackerel (successfully) is a whole story in itself. It can and is done with some regularity, but does require careful and thorough preparation.

- Tackle- Like most other kinds of fishing, individual preferences vary. While anything from 10-weight on up will work, more massive equipment is necessary if you're after a "Smoker" King. Two alternatives might include: 1) a 13-weight rod carrying an 850 grain shooting head, backed by 40 pound mono running line and plenty of Dacron backing on a narrow spooled, large diameter #5 Abel reel; and 2) a 13 weight rod carrying a number 10 intermediate line backed by Dacron on the large streel available from Islander.

- Approach- Anchor on bottom structure known to be frequented by Kings. Put out a block of frozen chum. Start spicing up your chum line with live bait. In the Panhandle area, Alewife, Menhaden and Cigar Minnows are effective. Once Kings show up, reduce the amount of live bait you're tossing to just what's required to keep the fish interested.

- Fly Pattern- A fly about the same size and silhouette as your live chum is ideal. Almost any Deceiver type pattern in white or white with a dark green or blue back should fool Mr. King. Whatever pattern you select, it should have eyes. Area experts seem to agree that eyes can trigger a strike.

- Rigging- You absolutely must use a short piece of light, coffee colored stainless wire about six inches long. Tie the wire directly to a doubled class tippet with an Albright Special, or use the tiniest black barrel swivel you can find. A haywire twist on the wire side of the swivel and a uni-knot on the tippet works just fine.

And that's the King Mackerel on a fly rod story. Sounds like a lot of work, but it really isn't...once your smoker

King is in the boat. Your feeling of accomplishment will far outweigh your prepatory efforts!

If you want additional information about salt-water fly-fishing in the *Panhandle* area, you're in luck. In the Destin area, there is a very active fly-fishing club called the Emerald Coast Flyrodders. The club has been in existence since 1985 and is affiliated with the Federation of Flyfishers. The club's founder Greg Miheve, is also a Master Fly Tier and outstanding source for quality saltwater flies- especially some of the newly publicized patterns. Greg can be reached by calling Greg's Custom Flies at 904-244-1602 or by writing to 507 Dory Ave., Fort Walton Beach, FL., 32548.

Panhandle Scalloping

In 1994, in an effort to salvage Florida's dwindling scallop population, the Marine Fisheries Commission closed almost all State waters to Bay Scallop harvesting. *Panhandle* waters, however, were and are a notable exception to the Commission's closure. The closure remains in effect today in the other parts of the state. The season is open in the *Panhandle* from July 1 to August 31.

Figure 4.3 - **Bay Scallop**

Bay scallops are bi-sexual, possessing both male and female reproductive characteristics. During the late Summer and Fall, scallops release sperm and then eggs. The resulting fertilized larvae attach themselves to seagrass blades after drifting around for a couple of weeks. They stay there 'til they're four to five months old. In the Spring, they drop off the grass onto the bottom, keep growing, and become mature and legal by mid-Summer. Out of the shell and ready to cook, Bay Scallops are about the size of a penny. Many believe they are far superior in taste to their much larger ocean relatives.

Harvesting Bay Scallops in any of the areas described below is incredibly easy and fun. In crystal clear waters usually five feet or less in depth, you simply pick them up off the bottom. The only equipment you might want is a snorkel and mask, a mesh bag and a dive flag on some kind of float. As noted earlier, the Bay Scallop season is open from July 1 through August 31. The daily bag limit is two gallons in the shell or one pint of meat per person. If you're scalloping out of a boat, the per person limits go away and a boat limit of 10 gallons in the shell or a half gallon of meat is in effect. Scallops can only be taken by hand or by using a dip net. Everyone over 16 must have a saltwater fishing license.

There are several spots in ***Panhandle*** waters where superb scalloping is available. Two of the best such spots are located in St. Joseph Bay and at the mouth of the Steinhatchee River. These spots are indicated by the stars on Figure 4.4. The waters around Keaton Beach are also consistently productive and worth checking out every year.

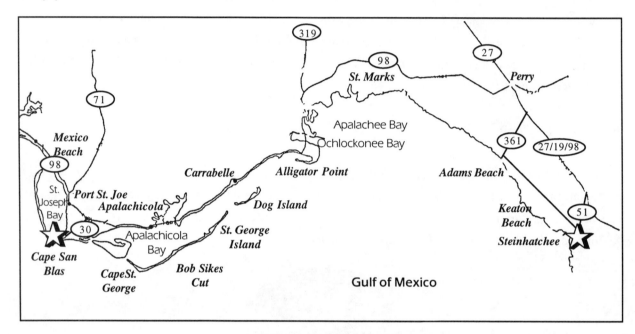

Figure 4.4 - ***Panhandle* Scalloping Spots**

St. Joseph Bay contains some 65 square miles of ragged marsh and island-flanked turtle grass flats. It is almost entirely enclosed inside a skinny 17 mile long peninsula. As noted in Chapter 3, the bay is home to many species of gamefish year round. In addition to its substantial Scallop population, several kinds of conch and left-handed whelks also populate the bay floor. Pen shells are another kind of shellfish found in St. Joseph Bay. For what its worth, many people actually prefer the sweet and tasty pen shell meat to that of the Scallop. Boats can be launched at the State Park midway up the North-South peninsula or at Presnell's Fish Camp on Highway 30. Good spots to try include the area inside Black's Island and on both sides of the State Park.

The Deadman Bay area at the mouth of the Steinhatchee River is another superb scalloping spot. According to knowledgable sources, the really good water starts at Pepperfish Keys, Northwest of Horseshoe and runs Westward from there. There are good boat ramps at Steinhatchee. A good public ramp may be found by crossing the bridge from Steinhatchee to Jena and then turning right. You'll run right into the ramp.

Besides being fun to catch, and like the Blue Crab discussed earlier, Scallops have a world-class reputation for "eatibility". But before you can do that, you've got to get the little rascals out of their shells. To do that, insert a scallop or table knife into the small gap at the back of the shell and cut the adductor muscle. Open the shell and then, with a circular cut, separate the slimy stuff from the firm, pale meat. Remove the edible meat from the other half of the shell--and you're almost ready to eat. First, a little cooking. Here are three recipes that just can't be beat.

Fried Scallops, St. Joe Bay Style

2 cups Scallops

½ cup flour

1 cup cracker meal or corn meal

1 egg

1 cup milk

½ tsp. garlic salt

1/4 tsp. pepper

1 Tbsp. Worcestershire sauce

"Beat together the Worcestershire sauce, egg and milk. Shake Scallops in a bag with the flour, garlic, salt and pepper. Dip Scallops in milk mixture, then roll in the meal until well coated. Drop into 350-degree fat in a frying pan. Remove as soon as they are golden brown--a couple of minutes at most. Drop only a few scallops at a time, being sure to maintain proper temperature of the grease."

Fast Seafood Fettuccine

2 pounds fettucine

3 packages McCormick's Pasta Prima Alfredo Sauce or similar product

3 pounds fresh peeled Shrimp

2 pounds fresh Scallops

1 stick butter

1 tbsp. olive oil

Everglades Seasoning

Lemon Pepper

Dill weed

Fresh grated Parmesan

Bring water to a boil and add tablespoon of olive oil. Boil fettucine until tender. Drain and set aside.

Saute Shrimp and Scallops separately until tender in large skillet with a half stick of butter. Add seasonings to taste. Set aside and keep warm. Prepare Alfredo sauce according to instructions on the package. Serve fettucine on a large platter, add sauce and sauteed shrimp and Scallops. Garnish with fresh grated Parmesan.

Coquilles St. Jacques

Coquilles St. Jacques is known to gourmets around the world as the creme de la creme of scallop recipes. Chefs at fancy restaurants would have you believe that there is some mystique to its preparation. True, it is not a quick dish to prepare. But, anyone who can chop and saute can make an admirable and delightful Coquilles St. Jacques. There are hundreds of variations, but basically this classic French dish consists of Scallops simmered in white wine and mixed with a fine, rich, cream sauce. They're then served in a Scallop shell, covered with bread crumbs and placed under a broiler to brown. Try it like this:

1 pound Scallops

4 scallions, thinly sliced

1 clove garlic, finely chopped

4 tsp. butter

10 fresh mushrooms, chopped

3/4 cup dry white wine

1 tsp. lemon juice

½ cup heavy cream

2 tsp. grated Parmesan cheese

1 tsp. flour

1 egg yolk

1/4 tsp. salt

1/8 tsp. pepper

3/4 cup bread crumbs

1/4 cup melted butter

"Rinse scallops in cold water and dry thoroughly. Saute the scallions and garlic in butter for five minutes. Add wine, lemon juice and Scallops. Simmer for four minutes or until Scallops just turn white. Do not overcook! Remove Scallops and set aside. Boil the remaining liquid until it is reduced by about half. Add the mushrooms and cool one minute. Mix the cream, Parmesan cheese, flour, egg yolk, salt and pepper, and add mixture to reduced liquid with mushrooms. Stir over low heat until mixture thickens. Remove from heat. Mix bread crumbs with melted butter. Place Scallops in large Scallop shells or individual baking dishes and place shells or baking dishes on a shallow baking pan. (One large casserole dish works fine too, if tradition is not your object.) Pour cream sauce over scallops and sprinkle bread crumbs on top. Place under broiler for five minutes or until top is lightly browned."

APPENDIX

FLORIDA SALTWATER RULES AND REGULATIONS

The following information has been tailored to fishing and related activities in the **Panhandle** area. State waters in this area extend nine miles out into the Gulf of Mexico and State rules and regulations apply. Beyond nine miles, Federal regulations are in effect. A table of applicable Federal size and bag limits is provided at the end of this appendix.

Before beginning this summary, a word of caution to the reader is important. Florida saltwater fishing rules and regulations have been and continue to be dynamic in nature. Sometimes, the rules change with almost no advance warning. Therefore, although the material contained in this appendix is current now (Summer '96), that may not be true a week or month from now. Smart fishermen monitor the rules closely over time--and avoid nasty surprises from our friendly Florida Marine Patrol!

The Fine Print

- **Who needs a saltwater fishing license?** Almost everybody who wants to catch saltwater fish. But there are exceptions. The following citizens do not need a license.
  - Anyone under 16 years of age (both resident and non resident)
  - Any Florida resident fishing from land or a structure fixed to the land (pier, bridge, dock, floating dock, jetty, or similar structure)
  - Anyone fishing from a boat that has a recreational vessel saltwater fishing license (**Panhandle** party, charter, and guide boats almost always have one).
  - Any Florida resident 65 years old or older
  - Anyone fishing from a pier that has been issued a pier saltwater fishing license (**Panhandle** area piers that charge an entrance fee have the required license).
  - Any Florida resident who is a member of the Armed Forces, not stationed in Florida, and home on leave for 30 days or less (your leave paper is required proof).

- **Who is considered a Florida Resident?**
  - Anyone who has continuously resided in the state for six months (owning, paying taxes on, and/ or periodically occupying a second/vacation home or rental property does not satisfy the requirement).
  - Anyone who has established a domicile in Florida and who has met the requirements of such law.
  - Anyone enrolled in a college or university in the state.

- **Where can I buy a license? How much do they cost?**
  - Any county tax collector's office and almost all bait and tackle stores sell licenses.
  - Resident licenses: 10 day for $10, one year for $12, and five years for $60.
  - Non Resident licenses: Three day for $5, seven day for $15, and one year for $30.
  - A tax collector's office adds a service charge of $1.50 to all licenses, commercial establishments add $2.

Other Rules of Interest/Relevance

- **Are there any saltwater fish I can't catch and keep?**
  - It is against the law to harvest, possess, land, purchase, sell or exchange the following fishes: Jewfish, Sawfish, Sawshark, Basking Shark, Whale Shark, Spotted Eagle Ray and Sturgeon.
- **Are there rules about tackle and fishing line?**
  - Yes. To help avoid entangling and injury of people as well as marine and shore life, hook-and-line gear must be tended at all times. It is against the law to intentionally discard any monofilament netting or line into or onto the waters of the State of Florida. Monofilament line can and does entangle birds, marine mammals, marine turtles, and other marine life, killing or injuring them.
- **Is it OK to use some kinds of traps?**
  - Yes. Traps may be used for recreational purposes for Stone Crab, Blue Crab, Shrimp, Pinfish and Black Seabass pursuant to the appropriate regulations.
- **What's the penalty for fishing without a license?**
  - Fifty dollars plus the cost of the applicable license or stamp.
- **Speaking of licenses, are there any special requirements associated with Tarpon fishing?**
  - Yes. A $50 special tag is required to kill or possess a Tarpon.
- **What's the law on displaying a "Diver Down" flag?**
  - Absolutely mandatory whenever you (or your kids regardless of age) are diving or snorkeling. For all kinds of very valid reasons, the Marine Patrol aggressively enforces this rule, particularly during Scalloping season.
- **Are treble hooks still legal for catching gamefish?**
  - Yes and No. Yes for all fish except Redfish, Black Drum, Pompano, and Trout. Treble hooks cannot be used with any kind of live or dead bait to catch these four species.
- **What are Florida size and bag limits?**
  - They're summarized in Figure A-1.

Fish	Min. Size (fork)	Min. Size (overall)	Max. Size (overall)	Daily Bag Limit
Amberjack	28 in.			3
Black Drum (1)		14 in.	24 in.	5
Blackfin Tuna		8 in.		
Bluefish	12 in.			10
Blue Marlin	86 in.			
Bonito				
Cobia	33 in.			2
Dolphin				
Flounder	12 in.			10
Grouper (3)		20 in.		5
Jack Cravalle				
King Mackerel	20 in.			2
Pompano	10-20 in.			10
Redfish		18 in.	27 in.	1
Sailfish (2)	57 in.			
Scamp (3)		20 in.		5
Sheepshead	12 in.			10
Snapper (Gray, Black, Mangrove) (4)		10 in.		5
Snapper (Mutton) (4)		16 in.		10
Snapper (Vermillion Mingo)		8 in.		
Snapper (Queen, Blackfin, Dog, Mahogany, Silk, Yellowtail) (4)		12 in.		10
Snapper (Red)		15 in.		5
Snapper (Schoolmaster)		10 in.		10
Spanish Mackerel	12 in.			10
Swordfish				10
Tarpon				2
Triggerfish (Gray)		12 in.		
Tripletail	15 in.			2
Trout (Speckled) (5)	15 in.		24 in.	7
Wahoo				
White Marlin (2)	62 in.			
Whiting				
Yellowfin Tuna				

Figure A-1 - **Florida Size and Bag Limits**

Notes

Blanks in the figure indicate no applicable specific limit. The numerical coding in the figure is explained below.

(1) One fish in the bag may be over 24 inches.

(2) Possession limit is one billfish (Blue Marlin, White Marlin, Sailfish or Spearfish). Length is measured from tip of lower jaw to fork of tail. It is illegal to buy or sell billfish.

(3) Minimum size applies to Black, Red, Gag, Scamp, Yellowmouth and Yellowfin Grouper; bag and possession to all Groupers in the aggregate, except one Warsaw Grouper per boat may be taken in addition to the aggregate limit. Nassau Grouper and Jewfish are closed to harvesting.

(4) Aggregate limits on Snapper are 10/day and 20 in possession. However, not more than 5/day and 10 in possession may be Gray/Black/Mangrove and not more than 2/day and 4 in possession may be Red. Lane and Vermillion (Mingo) Snappers are exempt from bag limits.

(5) Spec season is closed in the *Panhandle* area during the month of February. One of your seven trout may exceed 24 inches in length.

Florida Shellfish

- Clams, hard- Minimum size one inch in thickness; bag limit 2 bushels daily.
- Conch, Queen- Taking and possession prohibited.
- Corals, hard- Unlawful to take, damage or possess.
- Crab, Stone- Season open October 15 through May 15; size limit 2 3/4 inch forearm.
- Crawfish, (Spiny Lobster)- $2 Crawfish stamp is required by the state to harvest crawfish recreationally. Two day sport season covers the last consecutive Wednesday and Thursday of July. Regular season is August 6 through March 31. Minimum size- over 3 inch carapace or (on shore only) over 5 ½ inch tail. Bag limit in two day sport season is 6 per person daily in Monroe County, 12 per person daily in the rest of the state; state bag limit in regular season is 6 per person or 24 per boat daily, whichever is greater; and in Federal waters 6 per person daily. Other rules apply on harvest gear, diving times and measuring requirements.
- Oysters- Apalachicola Bay open all year; season closed elsewhere July 1 - September 30 (except in Dixie and Levy Counties where closed season is June 1 - August 31); minimum size, 3 inches; bag limit- 2 bags daily per person or vessel (whichever is less).
- Scallops, Bay- Season open July 1 - August 31, North and West of the Suwanee River only. Closed all year elsewhere, Bag limit; in shell- 2 gallons per person or 10 gallons per boat, whichever is less; cleaned meat- one pint per person or one-half gallon per boat, whichever is less.
- Shrimp- Daily bag 5 gallons (heads on) per person or vessel, whichever is less.

Federal Regulations

There are significantly fewer restrictions imposed in Federal waters than in State waters. Those relevant to the *Panhandle* area are summarized in the following figure and notes.

Fish	Min. Size (fork)	Min. Size (overall)	Bag Limit
Amberjack	28 in.		3
Cobia	33 in.		2
Grouper (1)		20 in.	5
King Mackerel	20 in.		2
Spanish Mackerel	12 in.		10
Blue Marlin (2)	86 in.		
White Marlin (2)	62 in.		
Sailfish (2)	57 in.		
Snapper (Lane and Vermillion)		8 in.	
Snapper (Red)		15 in.	5
Snapper (other) (3)		12 in.	10
Swordfish (4)	31 in.	41 lbs.	
Yellowfin Tuna	22 in.		

Figure A-2 - **Federal Size and Bag Limits**

Notes

(1) Minimum size applies to Black, Gag, Red, Yellowfin and Nassau Groupers; bag limit to all Groupers in the aggregate.

(2) Blue and White Marlin, Sailfish and Spearfish may not be sold.

(3) Minimum size applies to Gray, Mutton and Yellowtail Snappers; bag limit to all Snappers in the aggregate, excluding Red, Lane and Vermillion.

(4) Swordfish minimum weight is measured with the fish dressed and head and tail removed.

DON'T MISS ...

the rest of the *CATCH FISH NOW!* series

CATCH FISH NOW!
on
Florida's Northeast Coast

PANHANDLE

CATCH FISH NOW!
on
Florida's West Coast

CATCH FISH NOW!
on
Florida's Southeast Coast

CATCH FISH NOW!
in the
Ten Thousand Islands
and
Florida Keys

ABOUT THE AUTHOR ...

Mike Babbidge is a former Air Force Officer, aerospace industry executive, and independent consultant to the defense community. He has also been a life-long saltwater fishing fanatic. This has led to hands-on fishing experience in the central and south Atlantic, Caribbean Sea, Gulf of Mexico, Gulf of California, U.S. and Mexican Pacific coastal and offshore waters, Hawaii, and the South China Sea. In recent years, Mike has published numerous articles on Florida saltwater fishing. He is also the author of the best-selling book *CATCH FISH NOW! in the Destin Area.*

ABOUT THE AUTHOR'S WIFE ...

Sherry Babbidge has been recognized as one of their Top Sales Executives by the Prudential Real Estate companies of the Gulf Coast. Four years' real estate sales experience in the Southern California marketplace and almost seven years' Northwest Florida real estate sales have produced a consistent multi-million dollar record. Put her enthusiasm, experience and referral network to work for you. To find your very own **FLORIDA PANHANDLE** fishing place, please call Sherry at **800-862-1662+1662.**